CASENOTE® Legal Briefs®

PROFESSIONAL RESPONSIBILITY

Keyed to Courses Using

Gillers's
Regulation of Lawyers: Problems of Law and Ethics
Thirteenth Edition

Authored by: Publisher's Editorial Staff

ASPEN PUBLISHING

To contact Customer Service, e-mail customer.service@aspenpublishing.com, call 1-800-950-5259, or mail correspondence to:

Aspen Publishing
Attn: Order Department
1 Wall Street
Burlington, MA 01803

Printed in the United States of America.

1 2 3 4 5 6 7 8 9 0

ISBN 979-8-8890-6964-5

About Aspen Publishing

Aspen Publishing is a leading provider of legal educational content and digital learning solutions in the U.S. and around the world. Aspen provides best-in-class solutions through authoritative textbooks, written by renowned authors, and breakthrough products such as Connected eBooks, Connected Quizzing, PracticePerfect, and JD-Next.

The Aspen Casebook Series (famously known among law faculty and students as the "red and black" casebooks) encompasses hundreds of highly regarded textbooks in more than eighty disciplines, from large enrollment courses, such as Torts and Contracts, to emerging electives, like Sustainability and the Law of Policing. Study aids such as *Examples & Explanations* help law students master complex subject matter. Aspen's Paralegal, Criminal Justice, and Business Law series bring our hallmark publishing standards to undergraduate students. JD-Next is an innovative online law school prep course and admissions test that offers a realistic preview of law school, teaches underlying skills for academic success, and assesses applicants' academic readiness for law school.

Aspen Publishing is proud to be a UWorld company

Since 2003, UWorld has been a global leader in developing high-quality learning tools for students preparing for high-stakes exams. With a commitment to excellence, UWorld has helped millions of students in undergraduate, graduate, and professional programs in fields such as medicine, nursing, finance, and law achieve their academic and career goals.

Founded by Chandra S. Pemmasani, M.D., during his medical residency, UWorld began focusing on medical education and has since expanded into various academic fields, including law. In 2020, UWorld launched its Legal vertical, starting with its comprehensive Multistate Bar Exam (MBE®) Question Bank, followed by the acquisition of Themis Bar Review, which integrated resources to provide a complete bar exam preparation experience. In 2024, UWorld expanded its offerings by acquiring Aspen Publishing, enhancing its suite of legal education products.

Today, UWorld offers an unparalleled range of study materials that blend active learning methods with expert content, ensuring students and educators can access the most effective resources. From bar preparation to law school success, UWorld is committed to supporting the next generation of legal professionals. Learn more at uworld.com.

Format for the Casenote® Legal Brief

Nature of Case: This section identifies the form of action (e.g., breach of contract, negligence, battery), the type of proceeding (e.g., demurrer, appeal from trial court's jury instructions) or the relief sought (e.g., damages, injunction, criminal sanctions).

Fact Summary: This is included to refresh your memory and can be used as a quick reminder of the facts.

Rule of Law: Summarizes the general principle of law that the case illustrates. It may be used for instant recall of the court's holding and for classroom discussion or home review.

Facts: This section contains all relevant facts of the case, including the contentions of the parties and the lower court holdings. It is written in a logical order to give you a clear understanding of the case. The plaintiff and defendant are identified by their proper names throughout and are always labeled with a (P) or (D).

Issue: The issue is a concise question that brings out the essence of the opinion as it relates to the section of the casebook in which the case appears. Both substantive and procedural issues are included if relevant to the decision.

Palsgraf v. Long Island R.R. Co.

Injured bystander (P) v. Railroad company (D)

N.Y. Ct. App., 248 N.Y. 339, 162 N.E. 99 (1928).

NATURE OF CASE: Appeal from judgment affirming verdict for plaintiff seeking damages for personal injury.

FACT SUMMARY: Helen Palsgraf (P) was injured on R.R.'s (D) train platform when R.R.'s (D) guard helped a passenger aboard a moving train, causing his package to fall on the tracks. The package contained fireworks which exploded, creating a shock that tipped a scale onto Palsgraf (P).

RULE OF LAW

The risk reasonably to be perceived defines the duty to be obeyed.

FACTS: Helen Palsgraf (P) purchased a ticket to Rockaway Beach from R.R. (D) and was waiting on the train platform. As she waited, two men ran to catch a train that was pulling out from the platform. The first man jumped aboard, but the second man, who appeared as if he might fall, was helped aboard by the guard on the train who had kept the door open so they could jump aboard. A guard on the platform also helped by pushing him onto the train. The man was carrying a package wrapped in newspaper. In the process, the man dropped his package, which fell on the tracks. The package contained fireworks and exploded. The shock of the explosion was apparently of great enough strength to tip over some scales at the other end of the platform, which fell on Palsgraf (P) and injured her. A jury awarded her damages, and R.R. (D) appealed.

ISSUE: Does the risk reasonably to be perceived define the duty to be obeyed?

HOLDING AND DECISION: (Cardozo, C.J.) Yes. The risk reasonably to be perceived defines the duty to be obeyed. If there is no foreseeable hazard to the injured party as the result of a seemingly innocent act, the act does not become a tort because it happened to be a wrong as to another. If the wrong was not willful, the plaintiff must show that the act as to her had such great and apparent possibilities of danger as to entitle her to protection. Negligence in the abstract is not enough upon which to base liability. Negligence is a relative concept, evolving out of the common law doctrine of trespass on the case. To establish liability, the defendant must owe a legal duty of reasonable care to the injured party. A cause of action in tort will lie where harm, though unintended, could have been averted or avoided by observance of such a duty. The scope of the duty is limited by the range of danger that a reasonable person could foresee. In this case, there was nothing to suggest from the appearance of the parcel or otherwise that the parcel contained fireworks. The guard could not reasonably have had any warning of a threat to Palsgraf (P), and R.R. (D) therefore cannot be held liable. Judgment is reversed in favor of R.R. (D).

DISSENT: (Andrews, J.) The concept that there is no negligence unless R.R. (D) owes a legal duty to take care as to Palsgraf (P) herself is too narrow. Everyone owes to the world at large the duty of refraining from those acts that may unreasonably threaten the safety of others. If the guard's action was negligent as to those nearby, it was also negligent as to those outside what might be termed the "danger zone." For Palsgraf (P) to recover, R.R.'s (D) negligence must have been the proximate cause of her injury, a question of fact for the jury.

ANALYSIS

The majority defined the limit of the defendant's liability in terms of the danger that a reasonable person in defendant's situation would have perceived. The dissent argued that the limitation should not be placed on liability, but rather on damages. Judge Andrews suggested that only injuries that would not have happened but for R.R.'s (D) negligence should be compensable. Both the majority and dissent recognized the policy-driven need to limit liability for negligent acts, seeking, in the words of Judge Andrews, to define a framework "that will be practical and in keeping with the general understanding of mankind." The Restatement (Second) of Torts has accepted Judge Cardozo's view.

Quicknotes

FORESEEABILITY A reasonable expectation that change is the probable result of certain acts or omissions.

NEGLIGENCE Conduct falling below the standard of care that a reasonable person would demonstrate under similar conditions.

PROXIMATE CAUSE The natural sequence of events without which an injury would not have been sustained.

Party ID: Quick identification of the relationship between the parties.

Concurrence/Dissent: All concurrences and dissents are briefed whenever they are included by the casebook author.

Analysis: This last paragraph gives you a broad understanding of where the case "fits in" with other cases in the section of the book and with the entire course. It is a hornbook-style discussion indicating whether the case is a majority or minority opinion and comparing the principal case with other cases in the casebook. It may also provide analysis from restatements, uniform codes, and law review articles.

Holding and Decision: This section offers a clear and in-depth discussion of the rule of the case and the court's rationale. It is written in easy-to-understand language and answers the issue presented by applying the law to the facts of the case. When relevant, it includes a thorough discussion of the exceptions to the case as listed by the court, any major cites to the other cases on point, and the names of the judges who wrote the decisions.

Quicknotes: Conveniently defines legal terms found in the case.

Note to Students

Aspen Publishing is proud to offer *Casenote® Legal Briefs*—continuing thirty years of publishing America's best-selling legal briefs.

Casenote® Legal Briefs are designed to help you save time when briefing assigned cases. Organized under convenient headings, they show you how to abstract the basic facts and holdings from the text of the actual opinions handed down by the courts. Used as part of a rigorous study regimen, they can help you spend more time analyzing and critiquing points of law than on copying bits and pieces of judicial opinions into your notebook or outline.

Casenote® Legal Briefs should never be used as a substitute for assigned casebook readings. They work best when read as a follow-up to reviewing the underlying opinions themselves. Students who try to avoid reading and digesting the judicial opinions in their casebooks or online sources will end up shortchanging themselves in the long run. The ability to absorb, critique, and restate the dynamic and complex elements of case law decisions is crucial to your success in law school and beyond. It cannot be developed vicariously.

In addition to *Casenote® Legal Briefs*, Aspen Publishing offers the following study aids:

- *Casenote® Legal Briefs*
- *Emanuel® Law Outlines*
- Emanuel® *Law in a Flash* Flash Cards
- Emanuel® *CrunchTime®* Series

Each of these series is designed to provide you with easy-to-understand explanations of complex points of law. Each volume offers guidance on the principles of legal analysis and, consulted regularly, will hone your ability to spot relevant issues. We have titles that will help you prepare for class, prepare for your exams, and enhance your general comprehension of the law along the way.

To find out more about our law school tools for success, visit us at *www.AspenPublishing.com* or e-mail us at *customer.service@aspenpublishing.com*. We'll be happy to assist you.

How to Brief a Case

A. Decide on a Format and Stick to It

Structure is essential to a good brief. It enables you to arrange systematically the related parts that are scattered throughout most cases, thus making manageable and understandable what might otherwise seem to be an endless and unfathomable sea of information. There are, of course, an unlimited number of formats that can be utilized. However, it is best to find one that suits your needs and stick to it. Consistency breeds both efficiency and the security that when called upon you will know where to look in your brief for the information you are asked to give.

Any format, as long as it presents the essential elements of a case in an organized fashion, can be used. Experience, however, has led *Casenote® Legal Briefs* to develop and utilize the following format because of its logical flow and universal applicability.

NATURE OF CASE: This is a brief statement of the legal character and procedural status of the case (e.g., "Appeal of a burglary conviction").

There are many different alternatives open to a litigant dissatisfied with a court ruling. The key to determining which one has been used is to discover *who is asking this court for what.*

This first entry in the brief should be kept as *short as possible.* Use the court's terminology if you understand it. But since jurisdictions vary as to the titles of pleadings, the best entry is the one that addresses who wants what in this proceeding, not the one that sounds most like the court's language.

RULE OF LAW: A statement of the general principle of law that the case illustrates (e.g., "An acceptance that varies any term of the offer is considered a rejection and counteroffer").

Determining the rule of law of a case is a procedure similar to determining the issue of the case. Avoid being fooled by red herrings; there may be a few rules of law mentioned in the case excerpt, but usually only one is *the* rule with which the casebook editor is concerned. The techniques used to locate the issue, described below, may also be utilized to find the rule of law. Generally, your best guide is simply the chapter heading. It is a clue to the point the casebook editor seeks to make and should be kept in mind when reading every case in the respective section.

FACTS: A synopsis of only the essential facts of the case, i.e., those bearing upon or leading up to the issue.

The facts entry should be a short statement of the events and transactions that led one party to initiate legal proceedings against another in the first place. While some cases conveniently state the salient facts at the beginning of the decision, in other instances they will have to be culled from hiding places throughout the text, even from concurring and dissenting opinions. Some of the "facts" will often be in dispute and should be so noted. Conflicting evidence may be briefly pointed up. "Hard" facts must be included. Both must be *relevant* in order to be listed in the facts entry. It is impossible to tell what is relevant until the entire case is read, as the ultimate determination of the rights and liabilities of the parties may turn on something buried deep in the opinion.

Generally, the facts entry should not be longer than three to five *short* sentences.

It is often helpful to identify the role played by a party in a given context. For example, in a construction contract case the identification of a party as the "contractor" or "builder" alleviates the need to tell that that party was the one who was supposed to have built the house.

It is always helpful, and a good general practice, to identify the "plaintiff" and the "defendant." This may seem elementary and uncomplicated, but, especially in view of the creative editing practiced by some casebook editors, it is sometimes a difficult or even impossible task. Bear in mind that the *party presently* seeking something from this court may not be the plaintiff, and that sometimes only the cross-claim of a defendant is treated in the excerpt. Confusing or misaligning the parties can ruin your analysis and understanding of the case.

ISSUE: A statement of the general legal question answered by or illustrated in the case. For clarity, the issue is best put in the form of a question capable of a "yes" or "no" answer. In reality, the issue is simply the Rule of Law put in the form of a question (e.g., "May an offer be accepted by performance?").

The major problem presented in discerning what is *the* issue in the case is that an opinion usually purports to raise and answer several questions. However, except for rare cases, only one such question is really the issue in the case. Collateral issues not necessary to the resolution of the matter in controversy are handled by the court by language known as *"obiter dictum"* or merely *"dictum."* While dicta may be included later in the brief, they have no place under the issue heading.

To find the issue, ask *who wants what* and then go on to ask *why did that party succeed or fail in getting it.* Once this is determined, the "why" should be turned into a question.

The complexity of the issues in the cases will vary, but in all cases a single-sentence question should sum up the issue. *In a few cases,* there will be two, or even more rarely, three issues of equal importance to the resolution of the case. Each should be expressed in a single-sentence question.

Since many issues are resolved by a court in coming to a final disposition of a case, the casebook editor will reproduce the portion of the opinion containing the issue or issues most relevant to the area of law under scrutiny. A noted law professor gave this advice: "Close the book; look at the title on the cover." Chances are, if it is Property, you need not concern yourself with whether, for example, the federal government's treatment of the plaintiff's land really raises a federal question sufficient to support jurisdiction on this ground in federal court.

The same rule applies to chapter headings designating sub-areas within the subjects. They tip you off as to what the text is designed to teach. The cases are arranged in a casebook to show a progression or development of the law, so that the preceding cases may also help.

It is also most important to remember to *read the notes and questions* at the end of a case to determine what the editors wanted you to have gleaned from it.

HOLDING AND DECISION: This section should succinctly explain the rationale of the court in arriving at its decision. In capsulizing the "reasoning" of the court, it should always include an application of the general rule or rules of law to the specific facts of the case. Hidden justifications come to light in this entry: the reasons for the state of the law, the public policies, the biases and prejudices, those considerations that influence the justices' thinking and, ultimately, the outcome of the case. At the end, there should be a short indication of thedisposition or procedural resolution of the case (e.g., "Decision of the trial court for Mr. Smith (P) reversed").

The foregoing format is designed to help you "digest" the reams of case material with which you will be faced in your law school career. Once mastered by practice, it will place at your fingertips the information the authors of your casebooks have sought to impart to you in case-by-case illustration and analysis.

B. Be as Economical as Possible in Briefing Cases

Once armed with a format that encourages succinctness, it is as important to be economical with regard to the time spent on the actual reading of the case as it is to be economical in the writing of the brief itself. This does not mean "skimming" a case. Rather, it means reading the case with an "eye" trained to recognize into which "section" of your brief a particular passage or line fits and having a system for quickly and precisely marking the case so that the passages fitting any one particular part of the brief can be easily identified and brought together in a concise and accurate manner when the brief is actually written.

It is of no use to simply repeat everything in the opinion of the court; record only enough information to trigger your recollection of what the court said. Nevertheless, an accurate statement of the "law of the case," i.e., the legal principle applied to the facts, is absolutely essential to class preparation and to learning the law under the case method.

To that end, it is important to develop a "shorthand" that you can use to make marginal notations. These notations will tell you at a glance in which section of the brief you will be placing that particular passage or portion of the opinion.

Some students prefer to underline all the salient portions of the opinion (with a pencil or colored underliner marker), making marginal notations as they go along. Others prefer the color-coded method of underlining, utilizing different colors of markers to underline the salient portions of the case, each separate color being used to represent a different section of the brief. For example, blue underlining could be used for passages relating to the rule of law, yellow for those relating to the issue, and green for those relating to the holding and decision, etc. While it has its advocates, the color-coded method can be confusing and time-consuming (all that time spent on changing colored markers). Furthermore, it can interfere with the continuity and concentration many students deem essential to the reading of a case for maximum comprehension. In the end, however, it is a matter of personal preference and style. Just remember, whatever method you use, underlining must be used sparingly or its value is lost.

If you take the marginal notation route, an efficient and easy method is to go along underlining the key portions of the case and placing in the margin alongside them the following "markers" to indicate where a particular passage or line "belongs" in the brief you will write:

N	(NATURE OF CASE)
RL	(RULE OF LAW)
I	(ISSUE)
HL	(HOLDING AND DECISION, relates to the RULE OF LAW behind the decision)
HR	(HOLDING AND DECISION, gives the RATIONALE or reasoning behind the decision)
HA	(HOLDING AND DECISION, applies the general principle(s) of law to the facts of the case to arrive at the decision)

Remember that a particular passage may well contain information necessary to more than one part of your brief, in which case you simply note that in the margin. If you are using the color-coded underlining method instead of marginal notation, simply make asterisks or checks in the margin next to the passage in question in the colors that indicate the additional sections of the brief where it might be utilized.

The economy of utilizing "shorthand" in marking cases for briefing can be maintained in the actual brief writing process itself by utilizing "law student shorthand" within the brief. There are many commonly used words and phrases for which abbreviations can be substituted in your briefs (and in your class notes also). You can develop abbreviations that are personal to you and which will save you a lot of time. A reference list of briefing abbreviations can be found on page x of this book.

C. Use Both the Briefing Process and the Brief as a Learning Tool

Now that you have a format and the tools for briefing cases efficiently, the most important thing is to make the time spent in briefing profitable to you and to make the most advantageous use of the briefs you create. Of course, the briefs are invaluable for classroom reference when you are called upon to explain or analyze a particular case. However, they are also useful in reviewing for exams. A quick glance at the fact summary should bring the case to mind, and a rereading of the rule of law should enable you to go over the underlying legal concept in your mind, how it was applied in that particular case, and how it might apply in other factual settings.

As to the value to be derived from engaging in the briefing process itself, there is an immediate benefit that arises from being forced to sift through the essential facts and reasoning from the court's opinion and to succinctly express them in your own words in your brief. The process ensures that you understand the case and the point that it illustrates, and that means you will be ready to absorb further analysis and information brought forth in class. It also ensures you will have something to say when called upon in class. The briefing process helps develop a mental agility for getting to the *gist* of a case and for identifying, expounding on, and applying the legal concepts and issues found there. The briefing process is the mental process on which you must rely in taking law school examinations; it is also the mental process upon which lawyers rely in serving their clients and in making a living.

Abbreviations for Briefs

acceptance	acp
affirmed	aff
answer	ans
assumption of risk	a/r
attorney	atty
beyond a reasonable doubt	b/r/d
bona fide purchaser	BFP
breach of contract	br/k
cause of action	c/a
common law	c/l
Constitution	Con
constitutional	con
contract	K
contributory negligence	c/n
cross	x
cross-complaint	x/c
cross-examination	x/ex
cruel and unusual punishment	c/u/p
defendant	D
dismissed	dis
double jeopardy	d/j
due process	d/p
equal protection	e/p
equity	eq
evidence	ev
exclude	exc
exclusionary rule	exc/r
felony	f/n
freedom of speech	f/s
good faith	g/f
habeas corpus	h/c
hearsay	hr
husband	H
injunction	inj
in loco parentis	ILP
inter vivos	I/v
joint tenancy	j/t
judgment	judgt
jurisdiction	jur
last clear chance	LCC
long-arm statute	LAS
majority view	maj
meeting of minds	MOM
minority view	min
Miranda rule	Mir/r
Miranda warnings	Mir/w
negligence	neg
notice	ntc
nuisance	nus
obligation	ob
obscene	obs
offer	O
offeree	OE
offeror	OR
ordinance	ord
pain and suffering	p/s
parol evidence	p/e
plaintiff	P
prima facie	p/f
probable cause	p/c
proximate cause	px/c
real property	r/p
reasonable doubt	r/d
reasonable man	r/m
rebuttable presumption	rb/p
remanded	rem
res ipsa loquitur	RIL
respondeat superior	r/s
Restatement	RS
reversed	rev
Rule Against Perpetuities	RAP
search and seizure	s/s
search warrant	s/w
self-defense	s/d
specific performance	s/p
statute	S
statute of frauds	S/F
statute of limitations	S/L
summary judgment	s/j
tenancy at will	t/w
tenancy in common	t/c
tenant	t
third party	TP
third party beneficiary	TPB
transferred intent	TI
unconscionable	uncon
unconstitutional	unconst
undue influence	u/e
Uniform Commercial Code	UCC
unilateral	uni
vendee	VE
vendor	VR
versus	v
void for vagueness	VFV
weight of authority	w/a
weight of the evidence	w/e
wife	W
with	w/
within	w/i
without	w/o
without prejudice	w/o/p
wrongful death	wr/d

Table of Cases

Note: There are no principal cases in Chapter 1 of the casebook.

CHAPTER 2

Defining the Attorney-Client Relationship

Quick Reference Rules of Law

PAGE

1. *Office of Disciplinary Counsel v. Baldwin.* An attorney who represents a client before a grand jury violates the duty to provide competent representation where the attorney, who has no criminal law experience and has never represented a client before a grand jury, fails to appreciate the implications of the grand jury proceeding for the client, fails to consult with experienced counsel in this area, fails to prepare the client for the proceedings, fails to advise the client of their rights in the proceedings, and fails to conduct an independent investigation into available evidence relevant to potential charges the client might face. *2*

2. *Perez v. Kirk & Carrigan.* A lawyer may breach his fiduciary duty to maintain his client's confidences either by wrongfully disclosing a privileged statement or by disclosing an unprivileged statement after representing that it would be kept confidential. *5*

3. *Disciplinary Counsel v. Holmes & Kerr.* Where attorneys who work at separate firms and do not jointly represent any clients share their respective clients' confidential information, including information protected by the work-product doctrine or the attorney-client privilege, the attorneys have violated the professional rules of conduct prohibiting a lawyer from revealing information relating to the representation of a client, and from engaging in conduct that adversely reflects on the lawyer's fitness to practice law. *6*

4. *Upjohn Co. v. United States.* The attorney-client privilege between a corporation and its counsel extends to communications between counsel and noncontrol-level employees. *8*

5. *Taylor v. Illinois.* The client must accept the consequences of the lawyer's decision to forgo cross-examination, to not put certain witnesses on the stand, or to not disclose the identity of certain witnesses in advance of trial. *9*

6. *Yeschick v. Minetta.* It is not excusable neglect for an attorney in a lawsuit who is aware that their email address has been changed and that they are not receiving notices of electronic filings in their cases, to neither timely update their contact information on file with the court nor diligently monitor the docket in their client's case. *10*

7. *Nichols v. Keller.* An attorney may be obligated to alert a client to legal remedies outside the direct scope of that attorney's representation of the client. *12*

8. *Jones v. Barnes.* An attorney representing a defendant on appeal is not under a duty to raise every nonfrivolous issue requested by the defendant. *13*

9. *Olfe v. Gordon.* When a client's attorney disregards his or her client's instructions to the client's detriment, expert testimony is not required for the client to recover. *14*

Office of Disciplinary Counsel v. Baldwin

Attorney disciplinary board (P) v. Attorney (D)

Pa. Sup. Ct., 225 A.3d 817 (2020)

NATURE OF CASE: State's highest court's review of disciplinary board's petition for discipline of attorney for violations of state's rules of professional conduct. [The casebook extract focuses on violations of Rule 1.1, which requires competent representation.]

FACT SUMMARY: The state's Disciplinary Board (P) contended that Cynthia Baldwin (D), counsel for Penn State University, violated, inter alia, the state's professional conduct Rule 1.1 by failing to exercise the legal knowledge, skill, thoroughness, and preparation reasonably necessary for the representation of the university and three of its officials before a grand jury, and by failing to properly advise the clients and advocate on their behalf, to their detriment. Baldwin (D) contended that she did not do more for her clients because they asserted to her that they had committed no wrongdoing.

RULE OF LAW

An attorney who represents a client before a grand jury violates the duty to provide competent representation where the attorney, who has no criminal law experience and has never represented a client before a grand jury, fails to appreciate the implications of the grand jury proceeding for the client, fails to consult with experienced counsel in this area, fails to prepare the client for the proceedings, fails to advise the client of their rights in the proceedings, and fails to conduct an independent investigation into available evidence relevant to potential charges the client might face.

FACTS: Cynthia Baldwin (D) became General Counsel and Chief Legal Officer of Penn State University (Penn State) in 2010. Although she had served as a state trial judge and a member of Pennsylvania's Supreme Court, she had no criminal law experience and had never represented a client before a grand jury. In 2008, before Baldwin (D) began working for Penn State, a grand jury began investigating Jerry Sandusky, a famous Penn State football coach, for sexually abusing children. In 2011, in her capacity as counsel for Penn State, Baldwin (D) accompanied three Penn State officials who appeared before the grand jury. The three officials were Curley, Spanier, and Schultz. In preparation for the grand jury, Baldwin (D) did very little to prepare the clients as to what to expect or as to their rights, or even to the type of crimes to which they might be subjecting themselves if they did not assert the right against self-incrimination. Basically, she spent very little time with them in preparation and told them to tell the truth. She also did not seek the advice of outside counsel experienced with grand juries, nor did she conduct any independent investigations into how the three officials might be connected to Sandusky and how much they might have known about his alleged criminal activity. She did not seek any documents or electronically stored data, such as emails, that might be stored on Penn State's computers, which contained extensive archives of such data. Although the university itself had been served with a subpoena duces tecum to produce such data, and even though the university had in place a well-defined historical practice and procedure for responding to subpoenas, which involved information technology professionals who were trained and dedicated to assembling responsive electronically stored data for litigation needs or other legal processes, Baldwin (D) did not utilize any of these resources. Eventually, each official was convicted of endangering the welfare of minors, and Sandusky was convicted of sexually abusing 10 children. Based on these events, the state's Disciplinary Board and its Office of Disciplinary Counsel (ODC) (P) charged Baldwin (D) with violating several provisions of Pennsylvania's Rules of Professional Conduct, including Rule 1.1, which requires competence in the representation of clients. The ODC (P) petitioned the Pennsylvania Supreme Court to sanction Baldwin (D) for failing to exercise the legal knowledge, skill, thoroughness, and preparation reasonably necessary for the representation of the university and the three officials before the grand jury, and for failing to properly advise these clients and advocate on their behalf, to their detriment. Baldwin (D) asserted that she did not do more for the officials because they asserted to her that they had lied to her by insisting they had committed no wrongdoing. The court ruled that Baldwin (D) represented each of the officials individually, along with representing Penn State, before the grand jury, and considered the ODC's (P) petition.

ISSUE: Does an attorney who represents a client before a grand jury violate the duty to provide competent representation where the attorney, who has no criminal law experience and has never represented a client before a grand jury, fails to appreciate the implications of the grand jury proceeding for the client, fails to consult with experienced counsel in this area, fails to prepare the client for the proceedings, fails to advise the client of their rights in the proceedings, and fails to conduct an independent investigation into available evidence relevant to potential charges the client might face?

HOLDING AND DECISION: (Donohue, J.) Yes. An attorney who represents a client before a grand jury violates the duty to provide competent representation where the attorney, who has no criminal law experience and has never represented a client before a grand jury, fails to appreciate the implications of the grand jury proceeding for the client, fails to consult with experienced counsel in this area, fails to prepare the client for the proceedings, fails to advise the client of their rights in the proceedings, and fails to conduct an independent investigation into available evidence relevant to potential charges the client might face. The record shows that Baldwin (D) failed to exercise the legal knowledge, skill, thoroughness, and preparation reasonably necessary for the representation of her clients before the grand jury, and further failed to properly advise and advocate on their behalf, to their detriment. Baldwin (D) did not exhibit any understanding of the magnitude of the challenge that she was facing. She should have understood that by subpoenaing Curley and Schultz, the grand jury investigation was expanding beyond the conduct of Sandusky into the possible roles that individuals associated with Penn State may have had in facilitating or covering up his criminal acts, including, in particular, those that occurred on the Penn State campus. Their testimony potentially exposed Curley, Schultz, and Spanier to significant criminal liability, including prosecution for perjury, obstruction of justice, endangering the welfare of children, failure to report child abuse, and conspiracy. As representatives of Penn State, their testimony also potentially exposed the university to criminal liability as well as massive civil liability. She did not consult with expert counsel with experience with grand juries and criminal law, she did not review with the clients the types of questions that they were likely to be asked by the grand jury or how best to respond to any such questions, and she did not advise them of their rights to assert their rights against self-incrimination, or otherwise describe to them the nature and types of crimes to which they might be subjecting themselves if they did not assert this right. As to Baldwin's (D) assertion that she did not prepare more diligently in advance of the grand jury appearances because Curley and Schultz lied to her, misrepresenting that they were free of all wrongdoing, Baldwin (D) was simultaneously representing Penn State with regard to its response to the subpoena duces tecum, and, although it is questionable whether an attorney can ever blindly rely on statements by a client regarding events that occurred years prior to anticipated testimony, it was below any reasonable standard of care to do so here where another client, i.e., Penn State, may have been in possession of relevant documents. The duty to investigate becomes all the more important when, as here, counsel undertakes the representation of multiple clients, one of which is a sophisticated institutional client with massive document retention capabilities. Additionally, Baldwin (D) conducted little or no independent investigation prior to accompanying Curley and Schultz into the grand jury room. She did not, for instance, interview any members of their staff to inquire regarding their knowledge of prior Sandusky investigations, nor did she have anyone search their offices for relevant documents. Most importantly, prior to producing the clients for testimony before the grand jury, Baldwin (D) failed entirely to coordinate a search of any of the electronically stored data, including emails, on Penn State's computers; it is clear that information critical to her decision to represent simultaneously not only Penn State but also the three individual clients was at all times contained within the university's computer servers and available for extraction upon request. Even if, as Baldwin (D) claims, she had inadequate time to conduct such an investigation, at least for some of the clients, she could have requested a continuance but did not. In the absence of adequate time to investigate and garner any documents in the possession of Penn State regarding the Sandusky matters that were generated, received or reviewed by Curley, Schultz, and Spanier, Baldwin (D) could not conclude that the concurrent representation would be possible given that she had inadequate information upon which to make a conflict-of-interest analysis. Moreover, it was imperative for personal counsel for Curley, Schultz, and Spanier to fully investigate the available evidence to give competent advice on invoking the privilege against self-incrimination in testimony before the grand jury. For these reasons, Baldwin (D) failed to provide competent representation to clients in view of Rule 1.1. [Public reprimand ordered.]

ANALYSIS

In addition to concluding that the record clearly showed that Baldwin (D) had violated Rule 1.1, the court also ruled that she had violated Rule 1.6, which prohibits the disclosure of client confidences, and Rule 1.7, which obligates attorneys to avoid conflicts of interest. These findings show that attorneys cannot be experts in every area or aspect of the law, regardless of how long they have been admitted to practice, or how successful they have been in their career. After all, Baldwin (D) had served as a state trial judge, and, eventually, supreme court judge. Notwithstanding her experience as a judge, Baldwin (D) had no experience handling criminal matters or representing clients before a grand jury. As the court emphasized, she did not know enough to know what she didn't know or how to proceed. Thus, the case stands as an admonition to attorneys to know their own limitations and to seek assistance and advice when they take on a matter that is outside their areas of competence.

Quicknotes

GRAND JURY A group summoned to investigate, inform, and accuse persons of crimes when sufficient evidence exists to do so.

Continued on next page.

PENNSYLVANIA RULE OF PROFESSIONAL CONDUCT 1.1 Requires attorneys to provide competent representation of clients; competent representation requires the legal knowledge, skill, thoroughness, and preparation reasonably necessary for the representation.

PRIVILEGE AGAINST SELF-INCRIMINATION A privilege guaranteed by the Fifth Amendment to the U.S. Constitution in a criminal proceeding for communications made by an accused and protecting an accused or witness from having to give testimony that may incriminate themself.

Perez v. Kirk & Carrigan

Truck driver (P) v. Attorneys (D)

Tex. Ct. App., 822 S.W.2d 261 (1991)

NATURE OF CASE: Appeal from summary judgment in action for breach of fiduciary duty, infliction of emotional distress, and consumer protection violations.

FACT SUMMARY: After Perez's (P) truck accident claimed the lives of 21 children, lawyers Kirk & Carrigan (D) disseminated to the district attorney's office the confidential statements Perez (P) made to them, resulting in Perez's (P) indictment.

RULE OF LAW

A lawyer may breach his fiduciary duty to maintain his client's confidences either by wrongfully disclosing a privileged statement or by disclosing an unprivileged statement after representing that it would be kept confidential.

FACTS: Perez (P), a truck driver for the Valley Coca-Cola Bottling Company, was in a traffic accident that resulted in the deaths of 21 children. Kirk & Carrigan (D), lawyers hired to represent Valley Coca-Cola Bottling Company, visited Perez (P) the day after the accident in the hospital and told him they were his lawyers too. Perez (P) gave a sworn statement to Kirk & Carrigan (D) with the understanding that the statement would be kept confidential. Soon thereafter, Kirk & Carrigan (D) voluntarily disclosed Perez's (P) statement to the district attorney's office under threat of subpoena. The district attorney's office obtained an indictment for involuntary manslaughter against Perez (P) based upon the statement. Perez (P) brought an action for breach of fiduciary duty against Kirk & Carrigan (D). Kirk & Carrigan (D) moved for summary judgment on the ground that the attorney-client privilege did not apply to Perez's (P) statement. The trial court granted summary judgment, and Perez (P) appealed.

ISSUE: Does a lawyer breach his fiduciary duty to maintain his client's confidences either by wrongfully disclosing a privileged statement or by disclosing an unprivileged statement after representing that it would be kept confidential?

HOLDING AND DECISION: (Dorsey, J.) Yes. A lawyer breaches his fiduciary duty to maintain his client's confidences either by wrongfully disclosing a privileged statement or by disclosing an unprivileged statement after representing that it would be kept confidential. Perez's (P) allegation here that Kirk & Carrigan (D) breached their fiduciary duty owed to him when they voluntarily disseminated his statement to the district attorney's office was a valid claim for damages for the emotional distress and mental anguish he suffered after being indicted. Once an attorney-client relationship arose between Kirk & Carrigan (D) and Perez (P), Kirk & Carigan (D) had a fiduciary and ethical duty not to disseminate statements Perez (P) made to them in confidence, regardless of whether the statements were privileged or not. The relationship between attorney and client requires absolute and perfect candor, openness and honesty, and the absence of any concealment or deception. Perez (P) has made a valid claim for damages. [Reversed and remanded.]

ANALYSIS

It is important to note that much information that is ethically protected will not be privileged. However, virtually all information considered privileged under the Rules of Evidence will also be ethically protected. A lawyer whom a court orders to reveal information that is ethically protected but not privileged under the Rules of Evidence will be required to reveal the information under pain of contempt. But if that lawyer had voluntarily revealed the same information, he or she might be guilty of a disciplinary violation for failure to protect a client's secrets or confidences, unless revelation was for one of the purposes recognized by DR 4-101 or Rule 1.6.

Quicknotes

ATTORNEY-CLIENT PRIVILEGE A doctrine precluding the admission into evidence of confidential communications between an attorney and the client made in the course of obtaining professional assistance.

FIDUCIARY DUTY A legal obligation to act for the benefit of another, including subordinating one's personal interests to that of the other person.

Disciplinary Counsel v. Holmes & Kerr

Attorney disciplinary board (P) v. Attorneys (D)

Ohio Sup. Ct, 120 N.E.3d 820 (2018)

NATURE OF CASE: State's highest court's review of consent-to-discipline agreements for discipline of attorneys who violated state's rules of professional conduct.

FACT SUMMARY: Attorneys Thomas Holmes (D) and Ashleigh Kerr (D), who worked at separate firms and did not jointly represent any client, and who had a personal relationship, revealed confidential client information to each other. The state's disciplinary board (P) contended that they violated professional rules of conduct prohibiting a lawyer from revealing confidential client information, and from engaging in conduct that adversely reflects on the lawyer's fitness to practice law.

RULE OF LAW

Where attorneys who work at separate firms and do not jointly represent any clients share their respective clients' confidential information, including information protected by the work-product doctrine or the attorney-client privilege, the attorneys have violated the professional rules of conduct prohibiting a lawyer from revealing information relating to the representation of a client, and from engaging in conduct that adversely reflects on the lawyer's fitness to practice law.

FACTS: Attorneys Thomas Holmes (D) and Ashleigh Kerr (D), who worked at separate firms and did not jointly represent any client, met at a conference and started a personal relationship. Over the course of around two years, they exchanged emails in which they revealed client information to each other, including information protected by the work-product doctrine or the attorney-client privilege, mainly for the purpose of Holmes (D) assisting Kerr (D) with her work assignments. This conduct came to the state's disciplinary board's (P) attention after Holmes's (D) and Kerr's (D) respective firms discovered it, and, eventually, disciplinary counsel (P) charged Holmes (D) and Kerr (D) with violating the professional-conduct rules for improperly disclosing confidential client information. The board (P) considered the case on the parties' consent-to-discipline agreements, wherein the parties stipulated that Holmes (D) and Kerr (D) violated the professional rules of conduct prohibiting a lawyer from revealing information relating to the representation of a client, and from engaging in conduct that adversely reflects on the lawyer's fitness to practice law. As aggravating factors, the parties agreed that Holmes (D) and Kerr (D) each engaged in a pattern of misconduct. The stipulated mitigating factors were both attorneys' absence of prior discipline, cooperative attitudes toward the disciplinary proceedings, and evidence of good character. The parties recommended a stayed six-month suspension. The state's highest court considered whether to adopt the parties' consent-to-discipline agreements.

ISSUE: Where attorneys who work at separate firms and do not jointly represent any clients share their respective clients' confidential information, including information protected by the work-product doctrine or the attorney-client privilege, have the attorneys violated the professional rules of conduct prohibiting a lawyer from revealing information relating to the representation of a client, and from engaging in conduct that adversely reflects on the lawyer's fitness to practice law?

HOLDING AND DECISION: (Per curiam) Yes. Where attorneys who work at separate firms and do not jointly represent any clients share their respective clients' confidential information, including information protected by the work-product doctrine or the attorney-client privilege, the attorneys have violated the professional rules of conduct prohibiting a lawyer from revealing information relating to the representation of a client, and from engaging in conduct that adversely reflects on the lawyer's fitness to practice law. The parties' stipulations accurately reflect that Holmes (D) and Kerr (D) each engaged in a pattern of misconduct for close to two years. Based on precedent, a stayed suspension of six months is appropriate. The consent-to-discipline agreements are adopted.

ANALYSIS

The parties in this case stipulated that Holmes's (D) and Kerr's (D) misconduct was less egregious than the conduct of an attorney who had unnecessarily revealed attorney-client communications in a motion to withdraw as counsel, apparently in retaliation for the client's terminating the attorney without full payment—which merited a one-year suspension—but was more egregious that the conduct of an attorney who left 20 boxes containing confidential client files outside a dumpster near the attorney's former office—which merited a public reprimand. Because Holmes (D) and Kerr (D) each engaged in a pattern of misconduct for close to two years, the court agreed that a six-month suspension, albeit stayed, was appropriate given the degree of

Continued on next page.

egregiousness of their conduct as compared with the cases the parties cited.

Quicknotes

OHIO PROFESSIONAL CONDUCT RULE 1.6(A) Generally prohibits an attorney from revealing information relating to the representation of a client.

OHIO PROFESSIONAL CONDUCT RULE 8.4(H) Prohibits an attorney from engaging in conduct that adversely reflects on the lawyer's fitness to practice law.

STAYED SUSPENSION In the context of attorney disciplinary proceedings, a conditional postponement of the suspension of an attorney's license to practice law, allowing the attorney to render legal services if the attorney complies with certain conditions.

Upjohn Co. v. United States

Audited corporation (D) v. Internal Revenue Service (P)

449 U.S. 383 (1981)

NATURE OF CASE: Review of discovery order in tax investigation.

FACT SUMMARY: The Internal Revenue Service (IRS) (P), in a tax investigation of Upjohn Co. (D), sought disclosure of communications between middle- and lower-level employees and Upjohn's (D) attorneys.

RULE OF LAW

The attorney-client privilege between a corporation and its counsel extends to communications between counsel and noncontrol-level employees.

FACTS: The Internal Revenue Service (IRS) (P), in the course of a tax investigation of Upjohn Co. (D), sought disclosure of memoranda compiled by corporate attorneys during the course of their communications with nonsupervisory personnel. Upjohn (D) resisted, claiming the attorney-client privilege. The court of appeals held that the privilege applied only to communications between counsel and "control" employees, such as executives and senior management. The United States Supreme Court granted review.

ISSUE: Does the attorney-client privilege between a corporation and its counsel extend to communications between counsel and noncontrol-level employees?

HOLDING AND DECISION: (Rehnquist, J.) Yes. The attorney-client privilege between a corporation and its counsel extends to communications between counsel and noncontrol-level employees. The privilege exists largely because of recognition in the law that sound legal advice depends upon the lawyer being fully informed of relevant facts; if communications between a client and his counsel were discoverable, such communication would be largely circumscribed. In the context of a corporation, the information necessary for the corporation's attorneys to properly represent the corporation will not always come from the corporation's "control group"; often, the information will be in the possession of midlevel or even low-level employees. Communications between such employees and counsel may be no less necessary for proper representation, and therefore are no less deserving of confidentiality. Therefore, the privilege must be extended to all communications between counsel and corporate employees, no matter what level. Reversed.

ANALYSIS

It is important to note that the attorney-client privilege protects communications only, not information. While an attorney may not be compelled to disclose what a corporate attorney communicated to him, the privilege does not bar the party seeking discovery from obtaining the information from the employee through a recognized discovery procedure such as a deposition. While it would be more convenient for the IRS (P), for example, to simply subpoena the notes taken by Upjohn's (D) attorney, the court notes that considerations of convenience do not overcome the policies served by the attorney-client privilege.

Quicknotes

ATTORNEY-CLIENT PRIVILEGE A doctrine precluding the admission into evidence of confidential communications between an attorney and the client made in the course of obtaining professional assistance.

Taylor v. Illinois

Convicted criminal (D) v. Illinois (P)

484 U.S. 400 (1988)

NATURE OF CASE: Appeal from a criminal conviction.

FACT SUMMARY: Taylor (D) received a criminal conviction after the court refused to allow him to call a critical witness because his defense lawyer had failed to provide the prosecutor for the state of Illinois (P) with the name of the witness.

RULE OF LAW

The client must accept the consequences of the lawyer's decision to forgo cross-examination, to not put certain witnesses on the stand, or to not disclose the identity of certain witnesses in advance of trial.

FACTS: When Taylor's (D) lawyer refused to comply with the state prosecutor's (P) discovery request for the name of a witness pursuant to Illinois (P) discovery rules, the trial court judge refused to allow Taylor's (D) lawyer to call the witness whose testimony would have helped establish a defense of self-defense during the trial. Taylor (D) was convicted. Taylor's (D) conviction was upheld by the Illinois appellate courts, and Taylor (D) appealed to the United States Supreme Court, arguing that he should not be held responsible for his lawyer's misconduct.

ISSUE: Must the client accept the consequences of the lawyer's decision to forgo cross-examination, to not put certain witnesses on the stand, or to not disclose the identity of certain witnesses in advance of trial?

HOLDING AND DECISION: (Stevens, J.) Yes. The client must accept the consequences of the lawyer's decision to forgo cross-examination, to not put certain witnesses on the stand, or to not disclose the identity of certain witnesses in advance of trial. Taylor's (D) lawyer chose not to reveal his witness's identity until after the trial commenced. Taylor (D) has no right to disavow that decision now, absent ineffective assistance of counsel. Moreover, in responding to discovery, the client has a duty to be candid and forthcoming with the lawyer, and when the lawyer responds, he speaks for the client. Affirmed.

DISSENT: (Brennan, J.) In the absence of any evidence that a defendant played any part in an attorney's willful discovery violation, directly sanctioning the attorney is not only fairer but more effective in deterring violations than excluding defense evidence. While the court has sometimes held a defendant bound by tactical errors his attorney makes, we have not previously suggested that a client can be punished for an attorney's misconduct. There is no need to inflict punishment on the defendant because misconduct, not tactical errors, is amenable to direct punitive sanctions against attorneys as a deterrent that can prevent attorneys from systematically engaging in misconduct that would disrupt the trial process.

ANALYSIS

This case stands for the proposition that lawyers are their clients' agents. As such, the lawyer must have full authority to manage the conduct of his client's case because it would be impracticable to require client approval of every tactical decision a lawyer may make. Consequently, the lawyer's conduct will be attributable to the client, even if the lawyer errs or is careless.

Quicknotes

ATTORNEY-CLIENT PRIVILEGE A doctrine precluding the admission into evidence of confidential communications between an attorney and the client made in the course of obtaining professional assistance.

INEFFECTIVE ASSISTANCE OF COUNSEL A claim brought by an accused in which it must be determined whether the attorney's rendering of representation was such that the ultimate disposition of the case may not be relied upon as fair.

Yeschick v. Minetta

Former federal employee (P) v. Federal agency official (D)

675 F.3d 622 (6th Cir. 2012)

NATURE OF CASE: Appeal, on grounds of excusable neglect of counsel, from denial of motion for relief from judgment.

FACT SUMMARY: After Gary Yeschick's (P) lawsuit was terminated on summary judgment in favor of the opposing party, because Yeschick's (P) attorney had failed to check the court's docket and had failed to respond to the opponent's motion for summary judgment, Yeschick (P) sought relief from judgment on the grounds that his attorney's neglect was excusable.

RULE OF LAW

It is not excusable neglect for an attorney in a lawsuit who is aware that their email address has been changed and that they are not receiving notices of electronic filings in their cases, to neither timely update their contact information on file with the court nor diligently monitor the docket in their client's case.

FACTS: Gary Yeschick (P) brought suit against the Federal Aviation Administration (FAA) (D) in federal district court. The FAA (D) moved for summary judgment, but Yeschick's (P) attorney, Gino Pulito, neither received emails from the court clerk alerting him that the FAA (D) had moved for summary judgment, nor did he check the court system's internet-based docket. Pulito did not receive notice of the electronic filings because his email address had been changed by his Internet service provider, and he failed to update his email address on file with the court. However, he also did not check the docket in the case until more than a month after he learned (via communications regarding an unrelated case) that his email address was no longer working. Therefore, he missed the deadline for responding to the motion, and the district court granted the motion in the FAA's (D) favor. Yeschick (P) then filed a motion for relief from judgment on the grounds that Pulito's failure to receive notice of the filing of the summary judgment motion resulted in Pulito's failure to respond to the motion and constituted excusable neglect. The district court denied Yeschick's (P) motion, and Yeschick (P) appealed. The Sixth Circuit Court of Appeals granted review.

ISSUE: Is it excusable neglect for an attorney in a lawsuit who is aware that their email address has been changed and that they are not receiving notices of electronic filings in their cases, to neither timely update their contact information on file with the court nor diligently monitor the docket in their client's case?

HOLDING AND DECISION: (Gibbons, J.) No. It is not excusable neglect for an attorney in a lawsuit who is aware that their email address has been changed and that they are not receiving notices of electronic filings in their cases, to neither timely update their contact information on file with the court nor diligently monitor the docket in their client's case. Yeschick's (P) counsel's neglect in not checking the docket was not excusable, as parties have an affirmative duty to monitor the dockets. Now that electronic dockets are widely available, the burden imposed by this affirmative duty is minimal, since attorneys may monitor the docket from their computer. Further, email notification of docket activity is often available to assist attorneys in monitoring their cases. Regardless of the method of communication utilized (posted mail or email), it is the party, not the court, who bears the burden of apprising the court of any changes to their mailing address. Even looking beyond the basic duty to monitor the docket, the notice provided to Pulito about the problems with his email address in connection with the unrelated case should have given him at least some indication that action might have been taken in Yeschick's (P) case. It was within Pulito's control to update his contact information and to monitor the docket. Moreover, gross carelessness or inadvertent conduct that results in judgment will not give rise to a successful claim of excusable neglect if the facts demonstrate a lack of diligence. Here, Pulito's conduct demonstrated such a lack of diligence. [Affirmed.]

ANALYSIS

As this case illustrates, a litigant who invokes the processes of the courts is responsible for maintaining communication with the court during the pendency of their lawsuit, and clients are held accountable for their attorneys' acts and omissions. Thus, in assessing a claim of excusable neglect, the proper focus is upon whether the neglect of the parties *and their counsel* was excusable. The Supreme Court explained in *Pioneer Inv. Servs. Co. v. Brunswick Assocs. Ltd. P'ship,* 507 U.S. 380 (1993), that for purposes of a motion requesting relief from judgment, "excusable neglect" includes situations in which the failure to comply with a filing deadline is attributable to negligence. In *Pioneer*, the Supreme Court set forth five factors for determining whether neglect is excusable: the danger of prejudice to the non-moving party, the length of the delay and its potential impact on

Continued on next page.

judicial proceedings, the reason for the delay, including whether it was within the reasonable control of the movant, and whether the movant acted in good faith. However, these factors have been applied primarily in cases where procedural default has prevented the court from considering the true merits of a party's claim. Here, the district court, in granting summary judgment, had considered the merits of Yeschick's (P) claims. In such cases, the *Pioneer* factors are not controlling. Here, the courts focused on Pulito's duty to monitor the docket, and whether it was in Pulito's control to update his contact information with the court and monitor the docket.

Quicknotes

CM/ECF (CASE MANAGEMENT/ELECTRONIC CASE FILES) Part of federal judiciary's electronic docket system that allows case documents, such as pleadings, motions, and petitions, to be filed with the federal courts online.

DOCKET Log updated by a judge or clerk that contains the complete history of each case in the form of brief chronological entries summarizing the court proceedings, pleadings, motions, petitions, other filings, and deadlines.

FED. R. CIV. P. 60(B) Authorizes relief from judgment based on certain specified grounds.

PACER (PUBLIC ACCESS TO COURT ELECTRONIC RECORDS) Part of federal judiciary's electronic docket system that provides online public access to federal court records, with instantaneous access to more than one billion documents filed at all federal courts.

Nichols v. Keller

Injured employee (P) v. Workers' compensation attorneys (D)

Cal. Ct. App., 19 Cal. Rptr. 2d 601 (1993)

NATURE OF CASE: Appeal from summary judgment dismissing malpractice action.

FACT SUMMARY: Fulfer & Keller (D) contended that they had not been obligated to advise client Nichols (P) of his civil suit remedies following a work-related injury because they represented him only on his workers' compensation claim.

RULE OF LAW

An attorney may be obligated to alert a client to legal remedies outside the direct scope of that attorney's representation of the client.

FACTS: Nichols (P) suffered a job-related injury. He retained Fulfer & Keller (D) to represent him in a workers' compensation claim. He did not learn of his potential recourse against third parties by way of civil suit until after the statute of limitations had passed. He sued Fulfer & Keller (D) for malpractice, contending that they had been under a duty to advise him of his rights with respect to a third-party suit. The trial court granted summary judgment dismissing the action, holding that Fulfer & Keller (D) did not owe Nichols (P) any such duty as it was not within the course of their representation. Nichols (P) appealed.

ISSUE: May an attorney be obligated to alert a client to legal remedies outside the direct scope of that attorney's representation of the client?

HOLDING AND DECISION: (Martin, J.) Yes. An attorney may be obligated to alert a client to legal remedies outside the direct scope of that attorney's representation of the client. One of the attorney's basic functions is to advise. Advice need not be on every possible alternative, but should cover all foreseeable negative consequences. If such a consequence is foreseeable even in an area outside the attorney's scope of representation, the attorney is still under a duty to disclose the risk. He can then advise the client that it is outside his expertise and/or scope of representation and that the client should seek other counsel, and then the onus is placed on the client to protect his rights. However, until this is done, it is the attorney's responsibility to inform the client of such rights. Here, even though Fulfer & Keller (D) represented Nichols (P) only on his workers' compensation claim, a civil suit was sufficiently related to the scope of the representation that Nichols (P) should at least have been advised that the remedy existed. [Reversed.]

ANALYSIS

If there is one thing that gets lawyers in trouble with clients, it is lack of communication. Generally speaking, a lawyer can never disclose too much to a client; an attorney can, however, disclose too little, with consequences of the sort seen here. A good rule of thumb is "when in doubt, disclose."

Quicknotes

DUTY OF CARE A principle of negligence requiring an individual to act in such a manner as to avoid injury to a person to whom he or she owes an obligatory duty.

STATUTE OF LIMITATIONS A law prescribing the period in which a legal action may be commenced.

Jones v. Barnes

Public defender (D) v. Convicted robber (P)

463 U.S. 745 (1983)

NATURE OF CASE: Review of grant of habeas corpus.

FACT SUMMARY: Barnes (P) contended that he had an absolute right to have his attorney on appeal raise every nonfrivolous issue he requested.

RULE OF LAW

An attorney representing a defendant on appeal is not under a duty to raise every nonfrivolous issue requested by the defendant.

FACTS: Barnes (P) was convicted of armed robbery. A public defender was appointed to prosecute his appeal. Barnes (P) requested that certain issues be raised in the appeal. The attorney, for reasons of strategy, declined to press all the proffered issues. The conviction was affirmed. Barnes (P) petitioned for habeas corpus, contending that his attorney's refusal to prosecute all nonfrivolous issues constituted a denial of his Sixth Amendment right to counsel. The Second Circuit Court of Appeals granted the writ, and the United States Supreme Court granted review.

ISSUE: Is an attorney representing a defendant on appeal under a duty to raise every nonfrivolous issue requested by the defendant?

HOLDING AND DECISION: (Burger, C.J.) No. An attorney representing a defendant on appeal is not under a duty to raise every nonfrivolous issue requested by the defendant. It is safe to assume that counsel is in a better position than the defendant to assess how best to prosecute an appeal. In many situations, raising every issue will be detrimental to an appeal, as the weaker points will drown the stronger ones. To create a per se rule that a defendant is entitled to have appointed counsel raise every issue he wishes would seriously undermine the ability of counsel to present the client's case in accord with counsel's professional judgment. This court is unwilling to take such a step. Reversed.

CONCURRENCE: (Blackmun, J.) An attorney may be ethically bound to raise all nonfrivolous issues requested by the client, but this duty does not rise to constitutional status.

DISSENT: (Brennan, J.) An appeal ultimately belongs to the defendant, and he must have the final say in how it is prosecuted.

ANALYSIS

It must be remembered that this was a constitutional ruling. The court simply held that, as a matter of federal constitutional law, no right to press all issues on appeal belongs to one having appointed counsel. Depending on jurisdiction, an attorney may have an ethical obligation to prosecute all such issues. Canon 5 of the ABA Code of Professional Responsibility concerns an attorney's obligation to exercise independent professional judgment on behalf of such a client. This canon is primarily concerned with avoiding external, third-party influences over the attorney's decision-making process. It does not speak to interference by the client himself.

Quicknotes

HABEAS CORPUS A proceeding in which a defendant brings a writ to compel a judicial determination of whether he or she is lawfully being held in custody.

Olfe v. Gordon

Property seller (P) v. Real estate attorney (D)

Wis. Sup. Ct., 286 N.W.2d 573 (1980)

NATURE OF CASE: Appeal of dismissal of action against an attorney by his former client.

FACT SUMMARY: A trial court held that expert testimony was required for Olfe (P) to recover against her former attorney, Gordon (D), even though he had intentionally disregarded her instructions in the underlying transaction.

RULE OF LAW

When a client's attorney disregards his or her client's instructions to the client's detriment, expert testimony is not required for the client to recover.

FACTS: Olfe (P) retained Gordon (D), an attorney, to handle the sale of her house. She instructed him that she was willing to take back a first mortgage, but not a second mortgage. Nonetheless, Gordon (D) arranged a transaction that left Olfe (P) with a second mortgage, although Gordon (D) told her it was in fact a first mortgage. The purchaser defaulted, and the holder of the first mortgage foreclosed, extinguishing Olfe's (P) second mortgage. Olfe (P) lost about $25,000 and sued Gordon (D) to recover. After Olfe's (P) case, the court granted a nonsuit, on the basis that Olfe (P) had not provided expert testimony as to the standard of care required by attorneys in similar circumstances. Olfe (P) appealed.

ISSUE: When a client's attorney disregards his or her client's instructions to the client's detriment, is expert testimony required for the client to recover?

HOLDING AND DECISION: (Callow, J.) No. When a client's attorney disregards his or her client's instructions to the detriment of the client, expert testimony is not required for the client to recover. It has generally been recognized that an attorney may be liable for all losses caused by his failure to follow with reasonable promptness and care the explicit instructions of his or her client. Moreover, an attorney's honest belief that the instructions were not in the best interests of the client provides no defense to a suit for malpractice. The attorney-client relationship in such contexts is one of agent to principal, and an agent is answerable to that principal for failure to follow instructions. A cause of action in this situation may be based upon fiduciary principles, upon contract, or in tort. In any event, expert testimony is not needed, as a lay jury is perfectly capable of understanding on its own whether an attorney failed to follow instructions. [Reversed.]

ANALYSIS

The ABA Code of Professional Responsibility does not say in so many words that an attorney is duty-bound to follow his or her client's instructions. Canon 7 does require an attorney to represent a client zealously, but no mandate regarding instructions is made. The rule here is more a product of agency law than the code of ethics.

Quicknotes

AGENCY A fiduciary relationship whereby authority is granted to an agent to act on behalf of the principal in order to effectuate the principal's objective.

DUTY OF CARE A principle of negligence requiring an individual to act in such a manner as to avoid injury to a person to whom he or she owes an obligatory duty.

CHAPTER 3

Protecting the Attorney-Client Relationship Against Outside Interference

Quick Reference Rules of Law

	PAGE
1. *United States v. Carona.* Prosecutors do not violate their ethical obligations by communicating pre-indictment with an attorney-represented defendant through a cooperating witness who uses falsified documents provided by the prosecution to obtain evidence from the defendant.	*16*

United States v. Carona

Federal government (P) v. Corrupt sheriff (D)

660 F.3d 360 (9th Cir. 2011)

NATURE OF CASE: Appeal from conviction for witness tampering.

FACT SUMMARY: The district court held that federal prosecutors (P) violated Cal. R. Professional Conduct 2-100 by communicating with Carona (D), a former sheriff accused of various federal crimes and known by the prosecutors (P) to be represented by counsel, through Haidl, a cooperating witness, whom prosecutors (P) had given fake documents to use in eliciting incriminating statements.

RULE OF LAW

Prosecutors do not violate their ethical obligations by communicating pre-indictment with an attorney-represented defendant through a cooperating witness who uses falsified documents provided by the prosecution to obtain evidence from the defendant.

FACTS: Carona (D) had been the sheriff of Orange County, California, from 1999 to 2008, when he resigned after being indicted on various federal corruption charges. During his initial campaign for sheriff in 1998, Carona (D) received financial support from Haidl to whom Carona (D) had offered the complete power of the sheriff's department in exchange for raising money and supporting Carona (D). After Carona (D) was elected, Haidl continued to make illicit payments to Carona (D), and he also gave Carona (D) a speedboat, which they concealed via a sham transaction. The federal government (P) started an investigation into Carona's (D) corruption in 2004, and in 2007, Haidl admitted his guilt and signed a cooperation plea agreement with the government (P). Following this plea agreement, government attorneys (P) instructed Haidl to meet with Carona (D) and to make surreptitious recordings of their meetings. At this time, Carona (D) was represented by attorney Stewart, who had notified the government (P) that he was representing Carona (D). After two meetings between Haidl and Carona (D) that failed to yield adequate evidence, prosecutors (P) equipped Haidl with two fake "subpoena attachments" that identified certain records that Haidl was to tell Carona (D) he had been subpoenaed to produce. These documents referred to cash payments Haidl provided to Carona (D) and to the sham transaction they used to conceal the gift of the speedboat. At the next meeting between Haidl and Carona (D), Carona (D) made statements that suggested both that he had received payments and gifts from Haidl and that he wanted Haidl to lie to the grand jury about these transactions. Carona (D) was subsequently convicted of witness tampering. The district court, which had ruled that the prosecution (P) had violated Cal. R. Professional Conduct 2-100 by communicating with Carona (D) through Haidl, even though Carona (D) was known to be represented by counsel, nevertheless refused to suppress the evidence so obtained, instead leaving the matter for California's disciplinary authorities. The court of appeals granted review.

ISSUE: Do prosecutors violate their ethical obligations by communicating pre-indictment with an attorney-represented defendant through a cooperating witness who uses falsified documents provided by the prosecution to obtain evidence from the defendant?

HOLDING AND DECISION: (Clifton, J.) No. Prosecutors do not violate their ethical obligations by communicating pre-indictment with an attorney-represented defendant through a cooperating witness who uses falsified documents provided by the prosecution to obtain evidence from the defendant. Whether pre-indictment, non-custodial communications by federal prosecutors and investigators with represented parties violates Rule 2-100 is decided on a case-by-case basis. Precedent has more often than not held that specific instances of contact between undercover agents or cooperating witnesses and represented suspects do not violate Rule 2-100. The added wrinkle in this case is that here the prosecutors (P) provided Haidl with fake subpoena attachments to use in getting Carona (D) to incriminate himself. The district court held that this made Haidl the alter ego of the prosecutors (P), causing Haidl's communication with Carona (D) to violate Rule 2-100. The district court's ruling was erroneous because the use of the fake court papers did not cause Haidl to be any more an alter ego of the prosecutor (P) than he already was by agreeing to work with the prosecutor (P). The fake documents were mere props, and it has long been established that the government (P) may use deception in its investigations in order to induce suspects into making incriminating statements. The district court's concern that a suspect might be tricked by counsel's artful examination is inapplicable here, since Carona (D) was not subject to any interrogation, let alone one by the prosecutor (P). Rather he was engaging in a conversation with an individual he believed to be his ally. Finally, it would be antithetical to the administration of justice to allow a wrongdoer to immunize himself

Continued on next page.

against such undercover operations simply by letting it be known that he has retained counsel, especially where, as here, the defendant has encouraged others to lie to the grand jury. For all these reasons, as presented by the particular facts of this case, there was no violation of Rule 2-100. Affirmed.

ANALYSIS

The district court had based its finding that there had been a violation of the no-contact rule on the Second Circuit's decision in *United States v. Hammad,* 858 F.2d 834 (2d Cir. 1988), which held that issuing a false subpoena to an informant to "create a pretense that might help the informant elicit admissions . . . contributed to the informant's becoming that alter ego of the prosecutor." The court in this case, rejecting the *Hammad* rationale, concluded that the fake court papers did not render Haidl the prosecutor's (P) alter ego, reasoning that "If government officials may pose as non-existent sheiks in an elaborately concocted scheme, supply a necessary ingredient for a drug operation, and utilize landing strips, docking facilities, and other accouterments of an organized smuggling operation, all in order to catch criminals, then their use of a subpoena in the name of an undercover agent to enable him to retain his credibility with suspected criminals seems innocuous by comparison." No precedent from any circuit, with the exception of *Hammad,* has held such indirect contacts to violate Rule 2-100 or similar rules.

Quicknotes

ALTER EGO Other self; under the "alter ego" doctrine, the court disregards the corporate entity and holds the individual shareholders liable for acts done knowingly and intentionally in the corporation's name.

SUBPOENA A command issued by court to compel a witness to appear at trial.

CHAPTER 4

Lawyers, Money, and Legal Fees

Quick Reference Rules of Law

Brobeck, Phleger & Harrison v. Telex Corp.

Law firm (P) v. Computer corporation (D)

602 F.2d 866 (9th Cir.), *cert. denied*, 444 U.S. 981 (1979)

NATURE OF CASE: Appeal of award of damages for breach of contract.

FACT SUMMARY: Telex Corp. (D) contended that a contingency fee of $1,000,000 for the handling of a writ of certiorari to the United States Supreme Court was unconscionable.

RULE OF LAW

A contingency fee of $1,000,000 for handling a writ of certiorari to the United States Supreme Court is not unconscionable.

FACTS: Telex Corp. (D) filed an antitrust action against International Business Machines, Inc. (IBM). It recovered $259,500,000, but IBM recovered $18,500,000 by way of counterclaim. On appeal, the court of appeals reversed Telex's (D) award but affirmed that of IBM. Telex (D) engaged the firm of Brobeck, Phleger & Harrison (Brobeck) (P), a preeminent antitrust litigation firm, to handle a writ of certiorari to the Supreme Court. The fee arrangement called for a $25,000 retainer with a 5 percent contingency provision, the contingency in no event to be less than $1,000,000 in the event of a successful conclusion. [Telex (D) later denied that this had been the arrangement.] The petition was filed. Brobeck (P) eventually worked out a "wash" settlement wherein the writ would be dismissed in exchange for a dismissal of the counterclaim. Brobeck (P) then submitted a bill for $1,000,000, which Telex (D) refused to pay. Brobeck (P) sued for breach of contract. The district court awarded $1,000,000. Telex (D) appealed, contending that (1) the amount awarded did not reflect the terms of the contract, and (2) the amount of the contract was unconscionable.

ISSUE: Is a contingency fee of $1,000,000 for handling a writ of certiorari to the United States Supreme Court unconscionable?

HOLDING AND DECISION: (Per curiam) No. A contingency fee of $1,000,000 for handling a writ of certiorari to the United States Supreme Court is not unconscionable. [The court first decided that the award did in fact reflect the terms of the contract.] A contract will be unconscionable only if it is one that "no man in his senses and not under a delusion would make on the one hand, and no honest man would accept on the other." Such an analysis will naturally depend on the facts of the case. In this instance the client, Telex (D), was faced with a large judgment that apparently jeopardized its continued corporate existence. It engaged the services of a high-profile law firm, whose engagement was almost surely one of the reasons IBM was willing to dismiss its judgment in exchange for a dismissal of the certiorari petition. Under these circumstances, the retainer agreement cannot be said to fall within the test above. This is particularly true in light of the fact Telex (D) in no way could have been considered an unsophisticated client. Affirmed.

ANALYSIS

DR 2-106 of the ABA Code of Professional Responsibility provides, "A lawyer shall not enter into an agreement for, charge, or collect an illegal or clearly excessive fee." The Rule goes on to list certain factors to be considered in determining whether a fee is clearly excessive. Of particular importance was the factor enumerated in DR 2-106(B)(7): "[T]he experience, reputation, and ability of the lawyer or lawyers performing the services." In this instance, Telex (D) wanted and got the best, and for that it had to pay.

Quicknotes

PETITION FOR CERTIORARI A written request submitted to an appellate court asking that court to hear an appeal from an action in a lower court.

UNCONSCIONABILITY Rule of law whereby a court may excuse performance of a contract, or of a particular contract term, if it determines that such term(s) are unduly oppressive or unfair to one party to the contract.

Goldfarb v. Virginia State Bar

Real estate lawyers (P) v. State bar association (D)

421 U.S. 773 (1975)

NATURE OF CASE: Review of order dismissing class action seeking damages and injunctive relief under federal antitrust laws.

FACT SUMMARY: The Goldfarbs (P) contended that a minimum-fee schedule published by the Virginia State Bar (D) constituted price fixing in violation of the Sherman Act.

RULE OF LAW

Minimum fees mandated by a state bar may constitute price fixing in violation of the Sherman Act.

FACTS: The Goldfarbs (P) sought to engage a lawyer to do a title search on the home they wished to purchase. Per state law, only an attorney could do this. They consulted numerous attorneys, none of whom was willing to do the task for less than the minimum fee published by the Virginia State Bar (D). The Goldfarbs (P) subsequently brought a class action suit, contending that the minimum fee schedule constituted price fixing in violation of the Sherman Antitrust Act. The court of appeals held it was not, and dismissed. The United States Supreme Court granted review.

ISSUE: May minimum fees mandated by a state bar that constitute price fixing violate the Sherman Act?

HOLDING AND DECISION: (Burger, C.J.) Yes. Minimum fees mandated by a state bar may constitute price fixing in violation of the Sherman Act. To constitute a violation, the minimum fee schedule must amount to price fixing affecting interstate commerce, and not be subject to an exemption to the Sherman Act. A purely advisory fee schedule would present a different situation, but the record here reveals that attorneys in Virginia are under considerable pressure not to violate the State Bar's (D) fixed, rigid price floor. This being so, the schedule of minimum fees does constitute price fixing. It clearly affects interstate commerce. The State Bar (D) argues that an exception should be made for "learned professions." The problem with this argument is that no such exception exists in the Sherman Act. As the Act is expressly designed to reach as broadly as possible, courts should not create exceptions not found in the Act's text. Finally, the State Bar (D) argues that the fee schedule does fall within an exception for state action. The record here, however, belies this assertion. The State Bar (D) is not a governmental entity, but a private association to whom some regulatory oversight has been delegated. It is not an arm of either the executive or judicial branches of the state. If the state wanted to directly regulate fees, it could do so. It has not so done, however, so the exception is inapplicable. Therefore, since the fee schedule does constitute price fixing affecting interstate commerce and no exception applies, it violates the Sherman Act. Reversed and remanded.

ANALYSIS

In the 1970s, the United States Supreme Court began to whittle away at some of the powers that state bars once had to regulate the commercial aspect of lawyer behavior. Fee setting is an example. Another is lawyer advertising. Interestingly, Chief Justice Burger, who wrote the present opinion, was the most vociferous dissenter in the cases that liberalized lawyer advertising.

Quicknotes

MINIMUM FEE SCHEDULES The publication of recommended fee rates to be charged by attorneys; such fee schedules are in violation of federal antitrust laws.

STATE ACTION An action brought pursuant to the Fourteenth Amendment claiming that the government violated the plaintiff's civil rights.

CHAPTER 5

Concurrent Conflicts of Interest

Quick Reference Rules of Law

Cuyler v. Sullivan

[Party not identified] (P) v. Convicted murderer (D)

446 U.S. 335 (1980)

NATURE OF CASE: Review of habeas corpus granted subsequent to murder conviction.

FACT SUMMARY: Sullivan (D), convicted of murder, was granted habeas corpus because the court found the possibility of conflict in his representation.

RULE OF LAW

The mere potential of a conflict of interest in representation is not sufficient to invalidate a conviction.

FACTS: Sullivan (D) was accused of murder, along with two accomplices. Sullivan (D) was tried separately, his trial occurring first. He was represented by two attorneys, who also represented the accomplices. His attorneys rested without presenting evidence. Sullivan (D) was convicted. He appealed, contending that a conflict of interest existed as to his representation. The conviction was affirmed. Sullivan (D) petitioned for habeas corpus. At a hearing, one attorney testified that the decision not to present a case was due to a weak state case. The other testified that he didn't wish to reveal the testimony of certain witnesses, in view of the upcoming trial of the accomplices. The district court denied habeas corpus, but the court of appeals reversed, holding that since a possibility of conflict existed, Sullivan (D) had been denied effective counsel. The United States Supreme Court granted review.

ISSUE: Is the mere potential of a conflict of interest in representation sufficient to invalidate a conviction?

HOLDING AND DECISION: (Powell, J.) No. The mere potential of a conflict of interest in representation is not sufficient to invalidate a conviction. The potential for a conflict of interest exists in every situation involving multiple representation, so to hold that the mere potential of a conflict is sufficient to invalidate a conviction would end multiple representation. However, in many cases multiple representation actually improves the position of the defendant. In light of this, this court believes that only an actual conflict, as opposed to a potential conflict, should invalidate a conviction. Prejudice is presumed when a conflict exists but should not be when one is only possible. Vacated and remanded.

CONCURRENCE: (Brennan, J.) A court should undertake its own inquiry as to whether a conflict exists.

CONCURRENCE AND DISSENT: (Marshall, J.) The trial court has a duty to ascertain that multiple representation is the product of the defendant's informed choice.

ANALYSIS

No objection was made by Sullivan (D) to multiple representation in the underlying trial. In his habeas corpus petition, Sullivan (D) contended that a court should undertake its own investigation to determine the potential for conflicts. Justices Brennan and Marshall took exception to the court's ruling in this regard.

Quicknotes

CONFLICT OF INTEREST Ethical problems that arise, or may be anticipated to arise, between an attorney and the client if the interests of the attorney, another client, or a third party conflict with those of the present client.

HABEAS CORPUS A proceeding in which a defendant brings a writ to compel a judicial determination of whether he or she is lawfully being held in custody.

Wheat v. United States

Drug conspirator (D) v. Federal government (P)

486 U.S. 153 (1988)

NATURE OF CASE: Appeal from conviction for federal narcotics laws violations.

FACT SUMMARY: Ruling that a conflict existed, the district court refused to allow Wheat (D) to retain the same counsel who was representing Wheat's (D) codefendants.

RULE OF LAW

If a trial court believes that representation of a defendant by an attorney presents a serious potential for conflict, the court may refuse to permit that representation, even in the face of a waiver.

FACTS: Wheat (D) was indicted, along with Gomez-Barajas (D) and Bravo (D), for violation of federal narcotics laws. Shortly before his trial, Wheat (D) requested that the court allow him to substitute in as counsel of record Iredale, who also represented Gomez-Barajas (D) and Bravo (D), who had pleaded guilty but whose plea bargains had not as yet been accepted. The government (P) objected, contending that if the court elected not to permit Gomez-Barajas's (D) and Bravo's (D) plea bargains, Wheat (D) would almost certainly be called as witness at their subsequent trials. This would, said the government (P), put Iredale in conflict among his clients. Wheat (D) offered a waiver. Nonetheless, the court, finding strong probability of conflict, refused to allow Iredale to substitute in. Wheat (D) was convicted, and he appealed, contending he had been denied the right to counsel per the Sixth Amendment. The court of appeals affirmed, and the United States Supreme Court granted review.

ISSUE: If a trial court believes that representation of a defendant by an attorney presents a serious potential for conflict, may the court refuse to permit that representation, even in the face of a waiver?

HOLDING AND DECISION: (Rehnquist, C.J.) Yes. If a trial court believes that representation of a defendant by an attorney presents a serious potential for conflict, the court may refuse to permit that representation, even in the face of a waiver. The Sixth Amendment guarantees the right to effective counsel, not the right to counsel of choice. The guiding purpose behind the Amendment is to ensure a fair trial. While this goal has been interpreted to create a presumption in favor of permitting a party to retain counsel of choice, if the exercise of such choice leads to the potential for a fair trial to be unlikely, this presumption must give way. The possibility of waiver does not alter this conclusion. Courts have an interest in being sustained on appeal, and appellate courts can and do find waivers invalid in ineffective-assistance-of-counsel claims. The decision of whether to permit a representation that poses a threat of conflict is best made by the trial court, and nothing in the record here shows that the district court violated the standards articulated above. Affirmed.

DISSENT: (Marshall, J.) The propriety of the district court's order thus depends on whether the government (P) showed that the particular facts and circumstances of the multiple representation proposed in this case were such as to overcome the presumption in favor of a defendant's choice of counsel. It appears they were not.

DISSENT: (Stevens, J.) The court gives insufficient weight to the informed and voluntary nature of Wheat's (D) waiver.

ANALYSIS

The Sixth Amendment guarantees the right to counsel, but it is not absolute. It appears that the only certain right a defendant has regarding choice of representation is the right to waive counsel and represent himself, if he so chooses. This right was announced in *Faretta v. California*, 422 U.S. 806 (1975).

Quicknotes

CONFLICT OF INTEREST Ethical problems that arise, or may be anticipated to arise, between an attorney and the client if the interests of the attorney, another client, or a third party conflict with those of the present client.

SUBSTITUTION OF COUNSEL A situation in which a party seeks to terminate representation by a particular attorney or an attorney seeks to withdraw from a case; in order to substitute attorneys the party or attorney must obtain the court's permission, which may be denied if such substitution would result in an unfair delay or disruption of the proceedings.

People v. Adams

State (P) v. Alleged harasser (D)

N.Y. Ct. App., 987 N.E.2d 272 (2013)

NATURE OF CASE: Appeal from denial of motion to disqualify the district attorney's office as prosecutor.

FACT SUMMARY: Adams's (D) defense counsel filed a motion to disqualify the district attorney's office as prosecutor of charges against Adams (D) because of an alleged conflict of interest. The complainant was a sitting city court judge, and the district attorney's office, which appeared nearly daily in front of the judge, appeared to be handling Adams's (D) prosecution differently because of the complainant's status.

RULE OF LAW

The appearance of impropriety can be grounds for disqualification although the appearance must be of significance, and disqualification as a consequence is rare.

FACTS: Complainant, a sitting Rochester City Court judge, accused her neighbor and ex-paramour, Adams (D), of sending her three vulgar, hostile text messages by mobile phone. The messages had nothing to do with her status as a judge. Defendant was charged in Rochester City Court with two misdemeanor counts of aggravated harassment in the second degree. Assigned defense counsel withdrew and counsel from another county was appointed for Adams (D). Defense counsel spoke with the district attorney's office about a plea agreement, but the prosecutor stated the agreement, while fair, would not be offered because of the "position of the victim." Complainant insisted on going to trial. Adams's (D) counsel filed a motion to disqualify the district attorney's office on the basis of conflict of interest because the prosecutors regularly appeared before the judge and handled the proposed plea differently from every other similar case. [The County Court denied the motion and Adams (D) appealed.]

ISSUE: Can the appearance of impropriety be grounds for disqualification although the appearance must be of significance, and disqualification as a consequence is rare?

HOLDING AND DECISION: (Pigott, J.) Yes. The appearance of impropriety can be grounds for disqualification although the appearance must be of significance, and disqualification as a consequence is rare. Adams's (D) motion to disqualify the district attorney's office included an affidavit from original defense counsel stating the district attorney's office was handling this matter differently than any other similar prosecution solely because of the status of the complainant. Affiant argued the district attorney was forced to behave differently to avoid hostility from the judge before whom prosecutors appeared nearly daily. A similarly situated defendant should have received an adjournment in contemplation of dismissal (ACD) or violation with an Order of Protection. In response to the motion, the district attorney's office generally denied the conflict of interest allegation but did not provide an example of other cases in which it refused to offer a plea nor did it specifically rebut the allegation it consistently accepted pleas to reduced charges in similar cases. While rare, the appearance of impropriety can be grounds for disqualification. The appearance would have to be so great that public trust in the government and rule of law might be eroded. Here, it does not appear the prosecutor is reviewing the case based on its merits or legitimate prosecutorial concerns. There is no right to a plea agreement, but the appearance is that the prosecutor is refusing to offer a plea because the complainant is a sitting judge. The alleged crimes were not related to her judicial position nor were the charges that unusual for a harassment case. Nonetheless, despite prolonged negotiations, the district attorney's office did not offer reduced charges or agree to a plea. Former defense counsel stated he had never seen prosecutors take such a stance in similar cases and the district attorney's office did not respond to the disqualification motion with anything more than conclusory denials. This case involves a significant appearance of impropriety, which requires disqualification. Reversed.

ANALYSIS

Defendants do not have a legal right to reduced charges or a plea offer, but the public must be able to rely on prosecutorial fairness in evaluating similarly situated cases. Adams (D) did not prove the existence of a conflict of interest, but the evidence supported the significant appearance of a conflict of interest. Perhaps the prosecutors were not taking the judge's status into consideration, but it is better to remove even the scintilla of doubt so the public can be assured justice is blind.

Quicknotes

DISQUALIFICATION A determination of unfitness or ineligibility.

Fiandaca v. Cunningham

Female prison inmates (P) v. State (D)

827 F.2d 825 (1st Cir. 1987)

NATURE OF CASE: Appeal of injunction issued in action based on alleged equal protection violation.

FACT SUMMARY: A settlement offer made by the state of New Hampshire (D) to a class of plaintiffs was contrary to the interests of another client of the offeree's attorney.

RULE OF LAW

An attorney may not represent two clients when a settlement offer made to one is contrary to the interests of the other.

FACTS: A class of plaintiffs comprised of female inmates of the New Hampshire (D) penitentiary system brought action in which they claimed that they were denied equal protection because male inmates enjoyed superior facilities. They were represented by New Hampshire Legal Assistance (NHLA), a public-interest legal organization. NHLA also represented a class of students at a state school in an unrelated matter. At one point the state (D) offered to convert one of the school buildings into a penitentiary for women. The students represented by NHLA vehemently opposed this, and the convict plaintiffs rejected the offer. A trial ensued, and the district court held that the state penitentiary system denied equal protection to female convicts and ordered that a facility be built. The state (D) appealed, contending that the court should have disqualified NHLA from representing the plaintiff class.

ISSUE: May an attorney represent two clients when a settlement offer made to one is contrary to the interests of the other?

HOLDING AND DECISION: (Coffin, J.) No. An attorney may not represent two clients when a settlement offer made to one is contrary to the interests of the other. Rule 1.7 of New Hampshire's Rules of Professional Conduct prohibits an attorney from representing a client if the representation of that client may be materially limited by the lawyer's responsibilities to another client. Loyalty to a client is materially limited when a lawyer cannot recommend a possible course of action due to loyalty to another client. Thus, when a settlement offer is made and a lawyer owes allegiance to a party opposed to that settlement, that lawyer cannot use his independent judgment in advising the client. At this point a conflict exists. Here, NHLA could not recommend the state's (D) settlement offer because of a duty to another client, and it therefore should have been disqualified. [The court went on to affirm the finding of an equal protection violation, holding it not to have been tainted by the conflict, but ordered a retrial as to the remedy.] Vacated and remanded for a new trial.

ANALYSIS

It is usually possible for a potential conflict to be waived. This requires (1) a reasonable belief by the attorney that he can zealously represent both interests, and (2) a knowing consent by the affected parties. The court here, however, believed the conflict to be real, not potential.

Quicknotes

CLASS ACTION A suit commenced by a representative on behalf of an ascertainable group that is too large to appear in court, shares a commonality of interests, and will benefit from a successful result.

CONFLICT OF INTEREST Ethical problems that arise, or may be anticipated to arise, between an attorney and the client if the interests of the attorney, another client, or a third party conflict with those of the present client.

Simpson v. James

Restaurant owner (P) v. Attorney (D)

903 F.2d 372 (5th Cir. 1990)

NATURE OF CASE: Appeal of award of damages for professional malpractice.

FACT SUMMARY: Simpson (P), who retained Oliver (D) to represent her legally during the sale of her business, alleged that Oliver (D) committed malpractice by representing the buyers of her business as well.

RULE OF LAW

An attorney may commit malpractice by representing both sides in a transaction.

FACTS: Simpson (P) operated a restaurant, which she desired to sell. She contacted James (D), an attorney who had previously represented her, concerning a sale. Oliver (D), James's (D) partner, facilitated a transaction between Simpson (P) and Tide Creek, Inc. A deal was arranged wherein the business was sold for $500,000, $100,000 of which was paid down, with $400,000 payable in notes, secured by Tide Creek stock. The business proved unprofitable for Tide Creek, which eventually went bankrupt. Simpson (P) sued Oliver (D) and James (D), who had represented both sides in the transaction, contending that it had constituted malpractice for them to do so. A jury awarded Simpson (P) $200,000, and an appeal was made.

ISSUE: May an attorney commit malpractice by representing both sides in a transaction?

HOLDING AND DECISION: (Wisdom, J.) Yes. An attorney may commit malpractice by representing both sides in a transaction. While representing both sides is not inherently impermissible, it may make it difficult for an attorney to represent one side, the other, or both as zealously as professional standards require. Here, the jury found that James's (D) and Oliver's (D) failure to adequately safeguard Simpson's (P) pecuniary interests, such as creating a lien on Tide Creek's stock rather than the business's assets, proximately harmed Simpson (P). This was a permissible finding for the jury. [Affirmed.]

ANALYSIS

Upon examination, it can be concluded that dual representation didn't really figure into the result here, at least not directly. The malpractice was not a conflict of interest, although the conflict might have caused the behavior that constituted the malpractice. It would seem that an attorney who didn't represent the buyers would have been equally liable had he acted as did the defendants here. The facts given in the opinion do not shed light on whether the attorney would have acted differently absent the dual representation, so it is impossible to say whether the dual representation led to the malpractice.

Quicknotes

CONFLICT OF INTEREST Ethical problems that arise, or may be anticipated to arise, between an attorney and the client if the interests of the attorney, another client, or a third party conflict with those of the present client.

NEGLIGENCE Conduct falling below the standard of care that a reasonable person would demonstrate under similar conditions.

Note: There are no principal cases in Chapter 6 of the casebook.

CHAPTER 7

Ethics in Advocacy

Quick Reference Rules of Law

Nix v. Whiteside

[Party not identified] (P) v. Convicted killer (D)

475 U.S. 157 (1986)

NATURE OF CASE: Review of order granting habeas corpus subsequent to murder conviction.

FACT SUMMARY: Whiteside (D) contended that his counsel's refusal to allow him to commit perjury denied him his right to counsel.

RULE OF LAW

A criminal defendant is not denied his right to counsel if his counsel refuses to allow him to commit perjury.

FACTS: An altercation involving Whiteside (D) resulted in the stabbing death of another. Prior to testifying, Whiteside (D) told his attorney that he intended to state that he had seen a gun in the decedent's hand, even though he had previously stated to the contrary. The attorney informed him that to do so would constitute perjury, which he could not allow. The attorney informed Whiteside (D) that if he did so testify, he would inform the court of Whiteside's (D) perjury. Whiteside (D) did not so testify, and he was convicted of murder. He appealed, contending that counsel's threats to expose his perjury constituted a denial of counsel under the Sixth Amendment. This conviction was affirmed. Whiteside (D) petitioned for habeas corpus in district court. This was denied. The court of appeals reversed, agreeing with Whiteside's (D) contention. The United States Supreme Court granted review.

ISSUE: Is a criminal defendant denied his right to counsel if his counsel refuses to allow him to commit perjury?

HOLDING AND DECISION: (Burger, C.J.) No. A criminal defendant is not denied his right to counsel if his counsel refuses to allow him to commit perjury. The Sixth Amendment's right to counsel clause is not abridged unless counsel is so ineffective as to not have been functioning as counsel. It is the duty of the counsel to take all lawful measures to exonerate his client. However, counsel has no right to violate the law, or to assist others in doing so. Further, DR 7-102 of the ABA Code of Professional Responsibility prohibits an attorney from knowingly using perjured testimony or false evidence. Since counsel is not permitted to assist in perjury, it can hardly be considered ineffectiveness when he refuses to do so. Here, the only basis for Whiteside's (D) contention regarding ineffectiveness was the refusal to allow him to perjure himself, and therefore no Sixth Amendment violation occurred. Reversed.

CONCURRENCE: (Brennan, J.) The court can neither set rules of ethical conduct for lawyers practicing in the state courts nor enjoy statutory grants of jurisdiction over legal ethics.

CONCURRENCE: (Blackmun, J.) Whiteside's (D) argument is that he would have been acquitted had he been allowed to testify falsely. The answer to this is that the prevention of perjury can never be the basis for a conclusion that the trial was unfair, and therefore a defendant can never claim prejudice due to such prevention.

CONCURRENCE: (Stevens, J.) It should be remembered that recollections can and do augment themselves upon reflection, and the question is open as to how counsel should behave if it is not clear, as it was here, that perjury was in the offing.

ANALYSIS

It has never been affirmatively held that an accused has an absolute right to testify on his behalf. In fact, at one time an accused was categorically prohibited from such testimony. While not expressly approving such a right, the court here simply noted in passing that such a right is universally recognized.

Quicknotes

HABEAS CORPUS A proceeding in which a defendant brings a writ to compel a judicial determination of whether he or she is lawfully being held in custody.

PERJURY The making of false statements under oath.

State v. Bagby

State (P) v. Convicted felon (D)

Wash. Sup. Ct., 522 P.3d 982 (2023)

NATURE OF CASE: Appeal, on grounds of race-based prosecutorial misconduct, from affirmance of multiple felony convictions.

FACT SUMMARY: Tyler Bagby (D), an African-American citizen of the United States, was tried and convicted for multiple felonies. The judge, the lawyers, nearly all of the witnesses, and the entire jury panel were white. Bagby (D) contended that his convictions should be reversed because the prosecutor (P), in repeatedly asking witnesses to identify Bagby (D) by his "nationality," and, during closing arguments, in framing several white witnesses as "Good Samaritans" while conspicuously excluding the sole Black witness from such framing, notwithstanding that the Black witness did nothing to merit such exclusion, and, to the contrary, exemplified a "Good Samaritan," constituted race-based prosecutorial misconduct.

RULE OF LAW

A prosecutor commits race-based prosecutorial misconduct where the prosecutor flagrantly, or apparently intentionally, appeals to racial or ethnic bias in a manner that undermines the defendant's credibility or the presumption of innocence, thereby requiring a reversal of any conviction obtained by the prosecutor.

FACTS: Tyler Bagby (D), an African-American citizen of the United States, and a university student, went to a fraternity party one night with three friends, two of whom— Shyla Roberson and Kailah Crisostomo— were white, and one— Solomon Cooper— who was Black. An incident occurred in the bathroom that caused Bagby (D) to become enraged, and, when Austin Davis, a bystander, intervened and attempted to get Bagby (D) to leave the bathroom, Bagby (D) punched Davis, knocking him unconscious. Cooper eventually came to the bathroom and removed Bagby (D) from the party. Two witnesses, Sabrina Manzo and Leann Griffith, were present in the bathroom as these events unfolded. Further violence or threats of violence ensued as events deteriorated. In addition to the other witnesses, Elizabeth Nelson and Daniel Robinett witnessed the events. Bagby (D) was charged with multiple felonies. The case was tried by a jury. Bagby (D) was the only Black person at his trial other than Cooper. The judge, the lawyers, nearly all of the witnesses, and the entire jury panel were white. At trial, the prosecutor (P) called several witnesses to testify about what they saw during the incidents involved, and, in doing so, repeatedly asked witnesses to identify Bagby (D) by his "nationality," even though his nationality was irrelevant to the charges and not at issue in the case. The prosecutor (P) also referred to individuals as "the white guy" or "the Black guy," and continued to ask about individuals' nationalities. In some instances, when witnesses became confused by this question, the prosecutor (P) clarified he was asking about "ethnicity." Throughout the trial, neither party objected to questions or remarks about nationality, race, or ethnicity. Defense counsel also asked the witnesses to refer to the individuals involved by their nationality when describing what had occurred the night of the incidents. In closing arguments, the prosecutor (P) framed his argument around the theme, "This is a case with a bunch of [G]ood [S]amaritans. Mr. Bagby wasn't one of them." He proceeded to identify each witness one by one— Roberson, Davis, Manzo, Griffith, Nelson, and Robinett— as "[G]ood [S]amaritans." The prosecutor did not, however, identify Cooper— the person who helped remove Bagby (D) from the party and who tried to deescalate the situation— as a Good Samaritan. The prosecutor (P) described those other witnesses as "just regular folks who are going about their day hoping to have a good time at the party." The prosecutor (P) also repeatedly referred to Nelson and Robinett, two white witnesses, as "citizens," despite a lack of evidence in the record or other discussion regarding their citizenship status. The jury found Bagby (D) guilty of all but one of the charges. The state's intermediate appellate court affirmed, and the state's highest court granted review.

ISSUE: Does a prosecutor commit race-based prosecutorial misconduct where the prosecutor flagrantly, or apparently intentionally, appeals to racial or ethnic bias in a manner that undermines the defendant's credibility or the presumption of innocence, thereby requiring a reversal of any conviction obtained by the prosecutor?

HOLDING AND DECISION: (Montoya-Lewis, J.) Yes. A prosecutor commits race-based prosecutorial misconduct where the prosecutor flagrantly, or apparently intentionally, appeals to racial or ethnic bias in a manner that undermines the defendant's credibility or the presumption of innocence, thereby requiring a reversal of any conviction obtained by the prosecutor. Appeals to racial bias do not have to be express or blatant to trigger racial basis. Biases often can be activated through the use of coded language or racial code words such as phrases or symbols that play upon race and white Americans' negative views of Black Americans. When prosecutors

Continued on next page

utilize racially coded language, jurors respond with their own latent biases. Coded language often involves themes or euphemisms that evoke a conception of "us" versus "them." Terms such as "them," "these people," and "not like us" highlight the difference between the jurors and Black defendants and suggest that Black defendants are inherently different from white jurors and deserve less sympathy, thus interfering with jurors' ability to properly weigh evidence. Studies have shown that even the simplest racial cues can trigger implicit biases and affect the way jurors evaluate evidence, as well as impact juror decision-making more so than even explicit references to race. By calling attention to Bagby's (D) "nationality," the prosecutor (P) played into a stereotype that to be American is to be white and to be Black is somehow "foreign." By continuously referring to Bagby's (D) nationality, ethnicity, and race, the prosecutor (P) primed the all-white jury to pay more attention to this racial difference, thereby activating any anti-Black implicit biases the jurors may hold. In contrast to questions about Bagby's (D) nationality, the prosecutor (P) repeatedly used the term "citizens" to describe two white witnesses, thus further associating whiteness with being American and Blackness as un-American. This use of racial identifiers and frequent juxtapositioning of Black versus white further drew attention to Bagby's (D) race as a factor in the trial. Moreover, the prosecutor's (P) use of the term "nationality" or "ethnicity" served no purpose other than to emphasize Bagby's (D) race and produced a result that would have been the same had the prosecutor (P) used the term "race." Furthermore, the apparent purpose of the remarks about race and nationality was not to prove a relevant fact, nor was it based on evidence in the record. Bagby (D) is an American—his citizenship had absolutely nothing to do with the crimes he was charged with or the facts of the case. The pattern of treating white witnesses differently from Black witnesses continued in closing arguments, when the prosecutor (P) referred to the white witnesses as "Good Samaritans," but excluded Cooper as such—there was no apparent purpose based on the evidence in the record for why Cooper should have been singled out and excluded as a Good Samaritan, especially since it was Cooper who deescalated the situation. For these reasons, the prosecutor (P) engaged in race-based prosecutorial misconduct. [Conviction reversed.]

ANALYSIS

To prevail on a claim of race-based prosecutorial misconduct, a defendant must demonstrate that the prosecutor's conduct was both improper and prejudicial by showing that the prosecutor flagrantly, or apparently intentionally, appealed to racial or ethnic bias in a manner that undermined the defendant's credibility or the presumption of innocence. If the prosecutor's conduct meets this test, then the prosecutor's improper conduct is considered per se prejudicial, and reversal is required. Here, the court applied an objective observer standard of review, rather than using a subjective-based standard to discern the prosecutor's (P) subjective intent, to determine whether an objective observer could view the prosecutor's (P) questions and comments as an appeal to jurors' potential prejudice, bias, or stereotypes in a manner that undermined Bagby's (D) credibility or the presumption of innocence. Applying that objective standard, the court concluded that by intentionally and flagrantly tying the case to Bagby's (D) nationality, race, and ethnicity through repeated questioning about those topics, the prosecutor (P) had engaged in per se race-based prosecutorial misconduct. The pattern of treating white witnesses differently from Black witnesses continued in closing arguments, when the prosecutor (P) referred to the white witnesses as "Good Samaritans," but excluded Cooper as such – there was no apparent purpose based on the evidence in the record for why Cooper should have been singled out and excluded as a Good Samaritan.

Quicknotes

CLOSING ARGUMENT A lawyer's final opportunity in a trial to tell the jury and/or the judge why the lawyer should win the case, usually by explaining how the evidence supports the lawyer's theory of the case, and by clarifying for the jury any issues it must resolve to render a verdict.

PROSECUTORIAL MISCONDUCT Conduct by a prosecutor that is unlawful or otherwise improper and can result in a conviction being overturned or the prosecutor being disciplined.

Thul v. OneWest Bank, FSB

[Party not identified] (P) v. Banking institution (D)

2013 WL 212926 (N.D. Ill. 2013)

NATURE OF CASE: Court's order to show cause on sanctions against counsel.

FACT SUMMARY: Counsel for OneWest Bank, FSB failed to cite adverse precedent in their brief supporting their motion to dismiss Thul's (P) petition.

RULE OF LAW

Counsel is obligated to bring known adverse precedent to the court's attention.

FACTS: Three attorneys from Skadden, Arps, Meagher & Flom represented OneWest Bank, FSB (OneWest) (D). On behalf of their client, they moved to dismiss Thul's (P) petition. Counsel filed a brief in support of the motion and Thul's (P) counsel filed a brief in response. *Wigod v. Wells Fargo Bank, N.S.*, 673 F.3d 547 (7th Cir. 2012), was precedent directly adverse to OneWest's (D) position, but OneWest's (D) counsel failed to cite it in its brief. The court issued its order to show cause why counsel should not be sanctioned for its failure to cite the adverse case.

ISSUE: Is counsel obligated to bring known adverse precedent to the court's attention?

HOLDING AND DECISION: (Kennelly, J.) Yes. Counsel is obligated to bring known adverse precedent to the court's attention. Here, one of the attorneys was an associate who personally had no knowledge of *Wigod v. Wells Fargo Bank, N.S.*, 673 F.3d 547 (7th Cir. 2012), and relied on the briefing of the other two senior attorneys. The motion to show cause is vacated against him. The other two attorneys admitted their knowledge of *Wigod* and their failure to include it in their brief. They contend it is factually distinguishable, so they believed it did not need to be included. The court disagrees. The two, however, sincerely apologized to the court and to opposing counsel. Their firm has contributed financially to the interim settlement as a means of redressing Thul's (P) counsel expenses related to responding to the motion to dismiss. Also, the attorneys are named in the order to show cause, this order, and they were orally admonished during the hearing. The court will impose no further sanction.

ANALYSIS

It is not the job of opposing counsel to inform the court of adverse cases to a client's position. Each attorney has the affirmative obligation to inform the court of known adverse precedent. The attorney then can factually distinguish the case or argue why that law should be inapplicable in the present case. Failure to direct the court to all relevant cases, even ones that adversely impact one's client, can result in sanctions and ethics charges.

Quicknotes

SHOW CAUSE Generally referred to as an order to show cause or a show cause order. The order is directed to the opposing party to appear and show cause why a certain order should not be enforced or confirmed or give reason why a court should take or not take a proposed action.

CHAPTER 8

Special Issues in Criminal Cases

Quick Reference Rules of Law

In re Ryder

[N/A]

263 F. Supp. 360 (E.D. Va. 1967)

NATURE OF CASE: Court's own motion to suspend attorney from practice for criminal misconduct.

FACT SUMMARY: Ryder, an attorney, hid stolen money and a sawed-off shotgun belonging to his client in a safe-deposit box at his bank with the intention of keeping it there until after his client's trial for armed robbery.

RULE OF LAW

A defense attorney's withholding of incriminating evidence during a criminal proceeding for the purpose of hindering the preparation of the prosecution's case constitutes unethical deception and misconduct.

FACTS: Cook robbed a bank at gunpoint and deposited the proceeds as well as his sawed-off shotgun in a bank safe-deposit box. Some of the cash Cook obtained was "bait money," the serial numbers of which had been recorded. During an interview with the FBI, Cook turned over some of this "bait money," but called Ryder, an attorney who had represented him in a previous civil matter and asked him to attend the interview. Ryder did and had the agents leave. Cook then insisted he had not robbed the bank and had obtained the money at a crap game. Ryder telephoned one of the Federal Bureau of Investigation (FBI) agents, who told him that the serial numbers of the money Cook turned over matched some of those taken from the bank. Ryder then again asked Cook about the robbery, but Cook replied that on the day of the robbery a man had offered him $500 to put a package in a safe-deposit box. Ryder then consulted with various attorneys and judges in confidence about whether it would be proper to have a third party obtain the money in Cook's box and what would constitute a proper course of conduct thereafter. The advice of these lawyers was mixed and ambiguous. Ryder then asked Cook to execute a power of attorney authorizing access to Cook's safe-deposit box and authorizing him to dispose of its contents "as he saw fit" and "in a way that wouldn't harm Cook." Cook did so. Ryder then went to the bank and transferred the contents of Cook's box, the stolen money and the sawed-off shotgun, to a box in his own name. Ryder did not intend to notify the prosecution about this evidence, but only intended to turn it over if the government learned of it independently. Cook was then indicted for armed robbery, and FBI agents with search warrants for both Cook's and Ryder's boxes found Cook's contraband and weapon. The local federal district court then removed Ryder as Cook's counsel, suspended him from practice, referred the matter to the local U.S. Attorney, and set a hearing for further disciplinary proceedings against Ryder.

ISSUE: Does a defense attorney's withholding of incriminating evidence during a criminal proceeding for the purpose of hindering the preparation of the prosecutor's case constitute unethical deception and misconduct?

HOLDING AND DECISION: (Per curiam) Yes. A defense attorney's withholding of incriminating evidence during a criminal proceeding for the purpose of hindering the preparation of the prosecutor's case constitutes unethical deception and misconduct. Ryder took possession of the stolen money and sawed-off shotgun specifically to destroy the chain of evidence linking his client to the robbery. He intended to retain the evidence until at least after Cook's trial, unless the government first discovered it and compelled its production. Ryder knew that the money was stolen, that the man who robbed the bank used a sawed-off shotgun, that Cook's possession of the shotgun was illegal, and that his larceny was a continuing offense. He also knew that the laws against concealing stolen property and forbidding receipt and possession of a sawed-off shotgun contained no exemptions for lawyers. Thus, Ryder used the office of attorney in violation of the law in an effort to destroy an evidentiary presumption. Ryder would be disbarred were it not for two factors in mitigation: he intended to return the money after Cook's trial; and he consulted several attorneys before deciding on a course of conduct he may have believed constituted acting in the best interests of his client. Ryder was ordered suspended from the practice of law for 18 months.

ANALYSIS

The holdings of other cases are in accord with this decision. See, e.g., *People v. Superior Court (Fairbank)*, 192 Cal. App. 3d 32, 237 Cal. Rptr. 158 (1987) (a criminal defense lawyer must inform the court that he has taken possession of stolen property at issue in the criminal proceeding, even if it cannot be shown that the prosecution "needs" the evidence to prepare its case). See also *Commonwealth v. Stenbach*, 356 Pa. Super. 5, 514 A.2d 114 (1986), leave to appeal denied 517 Pa. 589, 534 A.2d 769 (1987) (lawyers are under an ethical obligation to turn over physical evidence to opposing counsel or to the court). Cf. N.Y. State Bar Committee on Professional Ethics, Opinion No. 479 (Mar. 6, 1978) (attorney whose

Continued on next page.

client was indicted for murder learned from the client the location of the bodies of victims of prior murders and actually took photographs of the bodies; it was held that it was not improper for the attorney to fail to reveal the location of the bodies or to use this knowledge with his client's approval in plea bargaining).

Quicknotes

ATTORNEY-CLIENT PRIVILEGE A doctrine precluding the admission into evidence of confidential communications between an attorney and the client made in the course of obtaining professional assistance.

POWER OF ATTORNEY A written instrument that allows a person to appoint an agent and confer authority to perform certain specified acts on his or her behalf.

People v. Meredith

State (P) v. Convicted robber and murderer (D)

Cal. Sup. Ct., 631 P.2d 46 (1981)

NATURE OF CASE: Appeal of conviction of robbery and murder.

FACT SUMMARY: An investigator working for criminal defendant Scott's (D) attorney observed and took possession of a wallet that had been taken from the victim and disposed of by Scott (D).

RULE OF LAW

The attorney-client privilege does not protect from disclosure testimony regarding observations made by counsel or counsel's agent concerning evidence that has been removed by counsel or the agent.

FACTS: Meredith (D) was charged with the robbery and murder of one Wade. Also charged was Scott (D). Scott (D) told Schenk, his counsel, that after Meredith (D) had killed Wade, Scott (D) took Wade's wallet and disposed of it in a trash container near Scott's (D) home. Schenk dispatched Frick, an investigator, to retrieve the wallet. Frick found the wallet and brought it to Schenk, who eventually turned it over to the prosecution. At trial, Frick was subpoenaed to testify about where he had found the wallet. The testimony was admitted over Scott's (D) attorney-client privilege objection. Scott (D) was convicted, and the state court of appeals affirmed. The California Supreme Court granted review.

ISSUE: Does the attorney-client privilege protect from disclosure testimony regarding observations made by counsel or counsel's agent concerning evidence that has been removed by counsel or agent?

HOLDING AND DECISION: (Tobriner, J.) No. The attorney-client privilege does not protect from disclosure testimony regarding observations made by counsel or counsel's agent concerning evidence that has been removed by counsel or the agent. Deciding this issue requires the balancing of competing considerations. On the one hand, to deny protection to observations arising from confidential communications could chill protected attorney-client communication. On the other hand, the privilege cannot be extended so far as to render immune from discovery evidence first obtained by the defense. It cannot be doubted that communications between counsel and his investigator are protected by the privilege. From this it is not a large step to conclude information acquired solely as a result of such communications are also protected. Here, Frick's knowledge of the location of the wallet was a result of information obtained from Schenk, so without more, introduction of testimony regarding his observations would be protected. However, when counsel or his agent takes the extra step of moving or altering the evidence, the opportunity of the prosecution to observe it is forever lost. To hold that testimony regarding the original state of the evidence cannot be compelled under these circumstances would effectively permit the defense to destroy critical evidence, a result not contemplated by the attorney-client privilege. Here, Frick did in fact remove the wallet, so the prosecution was properly permitted to question him concerning it. Affirmed.

ANALYSIS

Both the law and the Code of Professional Responsibility place a duty on attorneys with respect to evidence. As to testimonial evidence, an attorney may not facilitate perjury. As to tangible evidence, an attorney may not falsify the same. The subject is covered in Disciplinary Rule 7-102(A).

Quicknotes

ATTORNEY-CLIENT PRIVILEGE A doctrine precluding the admission into evidence of confidential communications between an attorney and the client made in the course of obtaining professional assistance.

DUTY OF CANDOR/DUTY OF FAIRNESS Ethical duty to turn over an instrumentality of crime once it has been used to aid a client's case, owed to the tribunal and opposing counsel to prevent the frustration of justice.

CHAPTER 9

Negotiation and Transactional Matters

Quick Reference Rules of Law

Greycas, Inc. v. Proud

Lender (P) v. Attorney (D)

826 F.2d 1560 (7th Cir. 1987)

NATURE OF CASE: Appeal of award of damages against an attorney under professional liability principles.

FACT SUMMARY: Greycas, Inc. (P) contended that Proud's (D) misrepresentations in his capacity as attorney to Crawford, a party adverse to Greycas (P), were actionable.

RULE OF LAW

An attorney may be professionally liable to one adverse to their client.

FACTS: Crawford was in dire need of capital for his farm business. He approached Greycas, Inc. (P) about a loan, offering his farm machinery as collateral. Upon Greycas's (P) demand, Crawford retained Proud (D), an attorney (and Crawford's brother-in-law), to draft a letter to the effect that he had performed a records search and was satisfied that the machinery had no prior security interests. This Proud (D) did, even though he had in fact conducted no search, and the machinery was subject to a prior security interest. Based on Proud's (D) assertions, Greycas (P) loaned over $1 million to Crawford. The following year, Crawford defaulted and committed suicide. Greycas (P), discovering that it had no security interest of any value, sued Proud (D). A district court, sitting in diversity, entered a judgment of $833,760 in Greycas's (P) favor. Proud (D) appealed, contending he owed no duty to Greycas (P).

ISSUE: May an attorney be professionally liable to one adverse to their client?

HOLDING AND DECISION: (Posner, J.) Yes. An attorney may be professionally liable to one adverse to their client. Courts long ago jettisoned concepts of contractual privity as requirements for liability, replacing them with more general concepts of duty. When the facts of a particular case are sufficient for the finding of such a duty, the adversarial or non-adversarial relationship of the parties is of little matter. In this particular case, Proud (D) made certain misrepresentations to Greycas (P), either intentionally or negligently, or both. The misrepresentations were intended to induce reliance and did in fact induce reliance on the part of Greycas (P), to Greycas's (P) detriment. Whether one considers this to be a case of professional liability or negligent misrepresentation or fraud does not matter. The bottom line is that, under the facts here, Proud (D) owed a duty of care to Greycas (P), which he breached. Affirmed.

ANALYSIS

The court here never quite made it clear to the reader whether it reached its conclusion based on professional liability principles or more general principles of misrepresentation. The court essentially admitted this to be the case, but disclaimed any importance thereto. This is not necessarily so, however. Whether the award was based on malpractice or misrepresentation could impact on the availability of insurance indemnification, as well as whether various professional rules of conduct could be implicated.

Quicknotes

DUTY OF CARE A principle of negligence requiring an individual to act in such a manner as to avoid injury to a person to whom he or she owes a duty.

FRAUD A false representation of facts with the intent that another will rely on the misrepresentation to his detriment.

MISREPRESENTATION A statement or conduct by one party to another that constitutes a false representation of fact.

PRIVITY Commonality of rights or interests between parties.

SECURITY INTEREST An interest in property that may be sold upon a default in payment of the debt.

Mok v. 21 Mott St. Restaurant Corp.

[Court (P) v. Plaintiff's attorney (D)]

2017 WL 3981308 (S.D.N.Y. 2017)

NATURE OF CASE: Ruling on sanctions against plaintiff's attorney.

FACT SUMMARY: The attorney for the plaintiff (D) in a wage and hour dispute failed to disclose to the court or opposing counsel that his client had died. The attorney (D) negotiated a settlement on his client's behalf and did not advise the court about the death until after he announced that he had reached an agreement-in-principle to settle. The court sought sanctions against the attorney (D) for his failure to disclose this material fact.

RULE OF LAW

A court's inherent power and 28 U.S.C. § 1927 permit the imposition of sanctions on an attorney who failed to disclose their client's death.

FACTS: Brandon Sherr (D), attorney for the plaintiff in a wage and hour dispute against his employer, did not disclose to the court or opposing counsel that his client had died until eight months after the client's death and four months after he learned of his client's death. Sherr's (D) client did not testify at a deposition, so Sherr (D) obtained adjournments from the court on the basis that he was negotiating with the client's employer on the client's behalf. The adjournments delayed the filing of a Joint Pretrial Order, which would have disclosed that Sherr's (D) client would not appear as a witness at trial. Sherr (D) did not disclose his client's death until after he announced that he and opposing counsel had reached an agreement-in-principle to settle. The court considered the New York Rules of Professional Conduct in determining whether Sherr (D) should be sanctioned under the court's inherent power and 28 U.S.C. § 1927.

ISSUE: Do a court's inherent power and 28 U.S.C. § 1927 permit the imposition of sanctions on an attorney who failed to disclose their client's death?

HOLDING AND DECISION: (Castel, J.) Yes. A court's inherent power and 28 U.S.C. § 1927 permit the imposition of sanctions on an attorney who failed to disclose their client's death. While a violation of the New York Rules of Professional Conduct (Rules) does not necessarily mean an attorney's conduct is sanctionable, the Rules can be relevant and useful in determining whether a lawyer acted in bad faith or unreasonably and vexatiously. Rule 3.3(a)(1) states that a lawyer shall not knowingly make a false statement of fact or law to a tribunal or fail to correct a false statement of material fact or law. Sherr (D) knowingly made a false statement when he told the court he was the lawyer for the plaintiff after the plaintiff had died. Rule 3.3(e) states that a lawyer shall disclose the identities of the clients he or she represents. Sherr (D) did not disclose that he had no client in the action, and instead stated that his client was the then-deceased plaintiff. Finally, New York Rule 3.4(a)(3) states that a lawyer shall not conceal or knowingly fail to disclose that which the lawyer is required by law to reveal. Sherr (D) was obliged to reveal his client's death, but failed to do so. Sherr (D) clearly acted in subjective bad faith and unreasonably and vexatiously prolonged the proceedings, unnecessarily caused defendants to incur attorneys' fees in negotiations, and took precious judicial time away from other litigants. Under the inherent power of the court. Sherr (D) will receive a monetary sanction of $3,000, and as a sanction under 28 U.S.C. § 1927, Sherr (D) will be required to pay defendants' legal fees from the date that he learned of his client's death. Sanctions imposed.

ANALYSIS

Brandon Sherr (D) is not the only attorney to receive sanctions for failing to disclose the death of a client. In the 2019 case of *In the Matter of Steven Pabros*, Case No. 17-O-05369, a California attorney received a thirty-day suspension and two years of probation for failing to disclose that his client, the defendant in a civil case, had died while the case was on appeal. The attorney failed to answer opposing counsel when asked why the defendant was not on the witness list at trial. Opposing counsel later learned of the defendant's death by performing an internet search.

Quicknotes

SANCTIONS A penalty imposed in order to ensure compliance with a statute or regulation.

CHAPTER 10

Lawyers for Companies and Other Organizations

Quick Reference Rules of Law

In re Grand Jury Subpoena: Under Seal

[N/A]

415 F.3d 333 (4th Cir. 2005)

NATURE OF CASE: Appeal from denial of motion to quash grand jury subpoenas.

FACT SUMMARY: Former employees of AOL (America Online) contended that grand jury subpoenas for documents related to an internal investigation conducted by AOL's attorneys should be quashed because the requested documents were protected by the attorney-client privilege and the joint defense privilege.

RULE OF LAW

(1) Conversations between a corporate employee and a corporation's attorneys during an internal investigation are not protected by the attorney-client privilege where the employee cannot show that an attorney-client relationship was formed during the investigation.

(2) Conversations between a corporate employee and a corporation's attorneys during an internal investigation are not protected by the joint defense privilege where the employee has entered into a common interest agreement with the company following the investigation.

FACTS: From March through June 2001, AOL (America Online) conducted an internal investigation into its relationship with PurchasePro, Inc. Outside counsel as well as in-house counsel conducted the investigation and interviewed AOL employees, including Wakeford, John Doe 1, and John Doe 2. The attorneys informed these employees that they represented AOL; that although the conversations were privileged, AOL could waive the privilege; and, if there was a conflict, the attorney-client privilege belonged to AOL. The attorneys also told the employees that either they could represent them, barring a conflict, or the employees could retain their own counsel, at AOL expense. In November, the Securities Exchange Commission (SEC) began to investigate AOL's relationship with PurchasePro. In December 2001, Wakeford and AOL, through counsel, entered into a "common interest agreement," which in part indicated that the disclosure of "Common Interest Materials" would not diminish the confidentiality of those materials or waive any applicable privilege. The employees testified before the SEC in 2002, and at their hearings, when questioned about their discussions with AOL attorneys during the March-June 2001 internal investigation, claimed that those discussions were protected by the attorney-client privilege. The employees indicated that they believed they were represented by the attorneys during those interviews. Two years later, a federal grand jury issued a subpoena commanding AOL to provide written memoranda and other written records reflecting the interviews of the employees conducted by the AOL attorneys from March to June 2001. AOL agreed to waive the attorney-client privilege and produce the subpoenaed documents, but the employees moved to quash the subpoena on the grounds that they each had an individual attorney-client relationship with the investigating attorneys, that their interviews were individually privileged, and that they had not waived the privilege. Wakeford also claimed that the information he disclosed to the investigating attorneys was privileged under the common interest doctrine. The district court denied the motions to quash, finding that in the case of all three employees none were clients of the investigating attorneys at the time of the interviews, and also denied Wakeford's motion on the ground that his common interest agreement with AOL postdated the interviews. The court based its conclusion on its findings that: (1) the investigating attorneys told the employees that they represented the company; (2) the investigating attorneys told the employees, "we represent you," not "we do represent you;" (3) the employees could not show that the investigating attorneys agreed to represent them; and (4) the investigating attorneys told the employees that the attorney-client privilege belonged to AOL and AOL could choose to waive it. The court of appeals granted review.

ISSUE:

(1) Are conversations between a corporate employee and a corporation's attorneys during an internal investigation protected by the attorney-client privilege where the employee cannot show that an attorney-client relationship was formed during the investigation?

(2) Are conversations between a corporate employee and a corporation's attorneys during an internal investigation protected by the joint defense privilege where the employee has entered into a common interest agreement with the company following the investigation?

HOLDING AND DECISION: (Wilson, J.)

(1) No. Conversations between a corporate employee and a corporation's attorneys during an internal investigation are not protected by the attorney-client

Continued on next page.

privilege where the employee cannot show that an attorney-client relationship was formed during the investigation. The essential elements for the formation of an attorney-client relationship between the investigating attorneys and the employees were missing at the time of the interviews. Despite the employees' subjective belief the attorneys were representing them personally, there was no evidence of an objectively reasonable, mutual understanding that the employees were seeking legal advice from the attorneys or that the attorneys were rendering personal legal advice. This conclusion is supported by the attorneys' disclosure to the employees that they represented AOL, and that the privilege and the right to waive it were AOL's alone. Moreover, the attorneys' statement to the employees that they could represent them absent a conflict was not a statement that they were representing them. In general, an individual's subjective belief that he is represented is not alone sufficient to create an attorney-client relationship. Instead, that subjective belief must be reasonable under the circumstances. Here, under the circumstances, the employees could not reasonably have believed that the investigating attorneys were representing them, given the attorneys' explicit disclaimers about AOL being their client, that the privilege belonged to AOL alone, and that they could, in theory, represent the employees (which in itself suggests that they were not representing the employees at the time of the interviews). In addition, the employees never asked the attorneys to represent them, nor did the attorneys offer to do so. Therefore, the district court did not err in finding that no attorney-client relationship was established at the time of the investigation, and, accordingly, the employees do not have a privilege that they can assert. Affirmed as to this issue.

(2) No. Conversations between a corporate employee and a corporation's attorneys during an internal investigation are not protected by the joint defense privilege where the employee has entered into a common interest agreement with the company following the investigation. The joint defense privilege is an extension of the attorney-client privilege and serves to protect communications between parties who share a common interest in litigation. The purpose of the privilege is to allow persons with a common interest to communicate with their respective attorneys and with each other to more effectively prosecute or defend their claims. For the privilege to apply, the proponent must establish that the parties had "some common interest about a legal matter." An employee's cooperation in an internal investigation alone is not sufficient to establish a common interest; rather "some form of joint strategy is necessary." The common interest agreement between AOL and Wakeford did not exist prior to December 2001, and these parties were not pursuing a joint legal strategy before that time. Also, during the time of the internal investigation, AOL would not have known whether its interests were aligned with, or adverse to, those of Wakeford. Accordingly, the district court did not err in concluding that Wakeford did not have a joint defense privilege during the investigation or any time before December 2001. Affirmed as to this issue.

ANALYSIS

If the investigating attorneys had in fact entered into an attorney-client relationship with the employees, they would not have been free to waive the employees' privilege when a conflict arose, since ethically they could not place one client's interests above those of another. Rather, the attorneys would have had to withdraw from all representation and to maintain all confidences. As the court itself observes, investigating counsel would not have been able to robustly investigate and report to management or the board of directors of a publicly traded corporation with the necessary candor if it were constrained by ethical obligations to individual employees. It is exactly for this reason that courts are reluctant to find that investigating attorneys who interview corporate employees or other corporate constituents form an attorney-client relationship with those interviewed. If they did, the investigating attorney would be faced with multiple conflicts and would be immobilized from conducting an investigation into wrongdoing.

Quicknotes

ATTORNEY-CLIENT PRIVILEGE A doctrine precluding the admission into evidence of confidential communications between an attorney and the client made in the course of obtaining professional assistance.

ATTORNEY-CLIENT RELATIONSHIP The confidential relationship established when a lawyer enters into employment with a client.

QUASH To vacate, annul, void.

SUBPOENA A command issued by court to compel a witness to appear at trial.

Tekni-Plex, Inc. v. Meyner & Landis

Manufacturing and packaging corporation (P) v. Attorneys (D)

N.Y. Ct. App., 674 N.E.2d 663 (1996)

NATURE OF CASE: Appeal over a corporate acquisition involving counsel's duties to the company and its sole shareowner.

FACT SUMMARY: Tang wanted to retain the same counsel his old corporation used after he had sold the corporation to another company. The new owners sought to disqualify this counsel.

RULE OF LAW

Counsel may not represent a present client against a former client involving matters that are substantially related to the prior representation and where the interests of the present client are materially adverse to the interests of the former client.

FACTS: Tom Tang was the president, chief executive officer, sole director, and sole shareholder of Tekni-Plex, Inc. Meyner & Landis (M&L) (D) represented Tang and Tekni-Plex on various legal matters, including securing an environmental permit for the operation of a laminator machine. Tang agreed to sell Tekni-Plex to the TP Acquisition Company (Acquisition). Acquisition was a shell corporation whose sole purpose was for the purchase of Tekni-Plex. Once the two corporations were merged Tekni-Plex would cease to exist and Acquisition would change its name to Tekni-Plex, Inc. (new Tekni-Plex) (P). Tang represented that old Tekni-Plex was in full compliance with all applicable environmental laws and possessed all requisite environmental permits. Tang and old Tekni-Plex were responsible for indemnification for any losses incurred by Acquisition as a result of misrepresentation. Following the merger, new Tekni-Plex (P) claimed that a laminator machine emitted volatile organic compounds and was therefore not allowed to operate. New Tekni-Plex (P) brought a claim against Tang for indemnification and Tang retained M&L (D) as counsel. New Tekni-Plex (P) sought to enjoin M&L (D) from representing Tang.

ISSUE: May counsel represent a present client against a former client involving matters that are substantially related to the prior representation and where the interests of the present client are materially adverse to the interests of the former client?

HOLDING AND DECISION: (Kaye, C.J.) No. Counsel may not represent a present client against a former client involving matters that are substantially related to the prior representation and where the interests of the present client are materially adverse to the interests of the former client. The court ruled that new Tekni-Plex (P) had the burden of satisfying a three-pronged test for the disqualification of M&L (D) (D). First, the court found that new Tekni-Plex (P) is a former client of M&L (D) since following the merger, the business of old Tekni-Plex remained unchanged and consequently control of the attorney-client privilege passed to the hands of the new Tekni-Plex (P) management. Second, the court found that there was a substantial relationship between the current and former representations since the current dispute concerned the merger agreement on which the law firm had represented old Tekni-Plex. Third, the court concluded that the interests of M&L's (D) present (Tang) client were materially adverse to the interests of its former client (Tekni-Plex) because the claim set the purchaser's interest against Tang's interest as the seller. Because of the inherent conflicts of interest, M&L (D) were disqualified from representing Tang. Judgment modified and affirmed.

ANALYSIS

Although the court found that new Tekni-Plex, Inc. (P) is a former client of Meyner & Landis (M&L) (D) since it is essentially the same as old Tekni-Plex, it prohibited M&L (D) from releasing certain communications to new Tekni-Plex (P). These communications included Tang's confidences to M&L (D) during the merger negotiations. Giving new Tekni-Plex (P) this information would cause a chilling effect between attorneys and their clients since clients would worry that their privileged communications with counsel might later become available to others.

Quicknotes

ATTORNEY-CLIENT PRIVILEGE A doctrine precluding the admission into evidence of confidential communications between an attorney and his client made in the course of obtaining professional assistance.

CONFLICT OF INTEREST Ethical problems that arise, or may be anticipated to arise, between an attorney and the client if the interests of the attorney, another client, or a third-party conflict with those of the present client.

DISQUALIFICATION A determination of unfitness or ineligibility.

Murphy & Demory, Ltd. v. Admiral Daniel J. Murphy, U.S.N. (Ret.)

Corporation (P) v. Former co-owner of corporation (D)

C.C. Va., Chancery No. 128219 (1994)

NATURE OF CASE: Legal malpractice action.

FACT SUMMARY: After Pillsbury (D), the law firm representing Murphy & Demory, Ltd. (P), assisted co-owner Murphy (D) in his efforts to take control of Murphy & Demory (P), Murphy & Demory (P) sued Pillsbury (D) for legal malpractice.

RULE OF LAW

Where dual representation of both a corporation and its individual owners presents a conflict of interest, the attorneys must obtain the corporation's consent for such representation after full disclosure of all material facts.

FACTS: Admiral Murphy (D) and Demory (P) co-owned Murphy & Demory, Ltd. (P). The law firm for Murphy & Demory Ltd. (P), Pillsbury, Madison & Sutro (Pillsbury) (D), through its attorneys Siemer (D) and Mendelson (D) assisted Murphy (D) in his efforts to take control of Murphy & Demory (P) or to form, before resigning from the company, a new corporation to compete with Murphy & Demory (P). Pillsbury (D) ignored its junior associates' warnings that the dual representation was rife with conflicts of interest, with possible breaches of fiduciary duty, and use of corporate opportunities. Murphy & Demory (P) filed suit against Admiral Murphy (D) and against Pillsbury (D).

ISSUE: Where dual representation of both a corporation and its individual owners presents a conflict of interest, must the attorneys obtain the corporation's consent for such representation after full disclosure of all material facts?

HOLDING AND DECISION: (Roush, J.) Yes. Where dual representation of both a corporation and its individual owners presents a conflict of interest, the attorneys must obtain the corporation's consent for such representation after full disclosure of all material facts. Here, Pillsbury (D) failed to disclose the conflict, to obtain consent for the dual representation of both Murphy (D) and Murphy & Demory, Ltd. (P), or, failing that, to withdraw from the representation. In concluding that there was no conflict, Siemer (D) willfully ignored the Rules of Professional Conduct. As a direct and proximate result of Pillsbury's (D) legal malpractice, Murphy & Demory, Ltd. (P) suffered compensatory damages in the amount of $500,000, and judgment is entered for that amount.

ANALYSIS

The court was particularly disturbed by the fact that every inquiry by an associate into the propriety of the firm's actions was referred to Siemer (D) for resolution. Siemer (D), the partner in charge of the client relationship affected by the issue, was the least likely to be objective, yet she was the ultimate arbiter of whether the firm had a conflict of interest. Mendelson (D) was held equally responsible for the legal malpractice since he was senior enough to have put a stop to the undisclosed dual representation.

Quicknotes

CONFLICT OF INTEREST Ethical problems that arise, or may be anticipated to arise, between an attorney and the client if the interests of the attorney, another client, or a third-party conflict with those of the present client.

FIDUCIARY DUTY A legal obligation to act for the benefit of another, including subordinating one's personal interests to that of the other person.

CHAPTER 11

Judges

Quick Reference Rules of Law

Caperton v. A.T. Massey Coal Co.

Business owner (P) v. Coal company (D)

556 U.S. 868 (2009)

NATURE OF CASE: Appeal from reversal of jury verdict for plaintiff in state tort action on grounds that failure of one of the reversing justices to recuse himself was an unconstitutional denial of due process.

FACT SUMMARY: A jury rendered a $50 million verdict against A.T. Massey Coal Co. and its affiliates (collectively, Massey) (D). Thereafter, the state was to hold its judicial elections. Massey's (D) chairman, Blankenship, became the largest contributor to Brent Benjamin's campaign for election to the state's highest court, and Benjamin was elected by a slim margin. Before the state's highest court was to hear the appeal in the case, Caperton and his affiliates (collectively, Caperton) (P) asked Benjamin to recuse himself based on the conflict caused by Blankenship's campaign involvement, but Benjamin refused, and continued to do so repeatedly. The state's highest court reversed the verdict. Caperton (P) asserted that Benjamin's failure to recuse himself was a due process violation.

RULE OF LAW

Due process requires recusal of an elected judge where the judge is deciding a case involving the interests of a contributor who by far made the largest financial contribution to the judge's election campaign and otherwise played a pivotal role in getting the judge elected, thus creating a "probability of bias."

FACTS: After a West Virginia jury found A.T. Massey Coal Co., a coal company, and its affiliates (collectively, Massey) (D), liable for fraudulent misrepresentation, concealment, and tortious interference with existing contractual relations and awarded Caperton, a business owner, and his affiliates (collectively, Caperton) (P) $50 million in damages, West Virginia held its 2004 judicial elections. The trial court denied Massey's (D) post-trial motions challenging the verdict and the damages award, finding that Massey (D) had intentionally acted in utter disregard of Caperton's (P) rights and ultimately destroyed Caperton's (P) businesses because, after conducting cost-benefit analyses, Massey (D) concluded it was in its financial interest to do so. Knowing the state's highest court, the West Virginia Supreme Court of Appeals, would consider the appeal, Blankenship, Massey's (D) chairman and principal officer, supported Brent Benjamin rather than the incumbent justice seeking reelection. Blankenship's $3 million in contributions exceeded the total amount spent by all other Benjamin supporters and by Benjamin's own committee. Benjamin won by fewer than 50,000 votes. Before Massey (D) filed its appeal, Caperton (P) moved to disqualify now-Justice Benjamin under the Due Process Clause and the state's Code of Judicial Conduct, based on the conflict caused by Blankenship's campaign involvement. Justice Benjamin denied the motion, indicating that he found nothing showing bias for or against any litigant. The state's Supreme Court then reversed the $50 million verdict. During the rehearing process, Justice Benjamin refused twice more to recuse himself, and the court once again reversed the jury verdict. Four months later, Justice Benjamin filed a concurring opinion, defending the court's opinion and his recusal decision. The United States Supreme Court granted certiorari.

ISSUE: Does due process require recusal of an elected judge where the judge is deciding a case involving the interests of a contributor who by far made the largest financial contribution to the judge's election campaign and otherwise played a pivotal role in getting the judge elected thus creating a "probability of bias?"

HOLDING AND DECISION: (Kennedy, J.) Yes. Due process requires recusal of an elected judge where the judge is deciding a case involving the interests of a contributor who by far made the largest financial contribution to the judge's election campaign and otherwise played a pivotal role in getting the judge elected, thus creating a "probability of bias." The Due Process Clause incorporated the common-law rule requiring recusal when a judge has "a direct, personal, substantial, pecuniary interest" in a case. In addition, there are other instances, as an objective matter, which require recusal where "the probability of actual bias on the part of the judge or decision maker is too high to be constitutionally tolerable." One instance involved local tribunals in which a judge had a financial interest in a case's outcome that was less than what would have been considered personal or direct at common law. Another involved a state supreme court justice who cast the deciding vote upholding a punitive damages award while he was the lead plaintiff in a nearly identical suit pending in the state's lower courts. The proper constitutional inquiry was not "whether in fact [the justice] was influenced," but "whether sitting on [that] case . . . 'would offer a possible temptation to the average . . . judge to . . . lead him not to hold the balance nice, clear and true.'" Still another instance emerged in the criminal contempt context, where a judge had no pecuniary interest in the case but had determined in an

Continued on next page.

earlier proceeding whether criminal charges should be brought and then proceeded to try and convict the petitioners. In this regard, the court has said "no man can be a judge in his own case," and "no man is permitted to try cases where he has an interest in the outcome." The judge's prior relationship with the defendant, as well as the information acquired from the prior proceeding, was critical. In reiterating that the rule that "a defendant in criminal contempt proceedings should be [tried] before a judge other than the one reviled by the contemnor," the court noted that the objective inquiry is not whether the judge is actually biased, but whether the average judge in his position is likely to be neutral or there is an unconstitutional "potential for bias." Because the objective standards implementing the Due Process Clause do not require proof of actual bias Justice Benjamin's subjective findings of impartiality and propriety are not questioned, and there is no need to determine whether there was actual bias. Rather, the question is whether, "under a realistic appraisal of psychological tendencies and human weakness," the interest "poses such a risk of actual bias or prejudgment that the practice must be forbidden if the guarantee of due process is to be adequately implemented." Applying these principles here, there is a serious risk of actual bias when a person with a personal stake in a particular case had a significant and disproportionate influence in placing the judge on the case by raising funds or directing the judge's election campaign when the case was pending or imminent. The proper inquiry centers on the contribution's relative size in comparison to the total amount contributed to the campaign, the total amount spent in the election, and the apparent effect of the contribution on the outcome. It is not whether the contributions were a necessary and sufficient cause of Benjamin's victory. In an election decided by fewer than 50,000 votes, Blankenship's campaign contributions—compared to the total amount contributed to the campaign, as well as the total amount spent in the election—had a significant and disproportionate influence on the outcome. The risk that Blankenship's influence engendered actual bias is sufficiently substantial that it "must be forbidden if the guarantee of due process is to be adequately implemented." The temporal relationship between the campaign contributions, the justice's election, and the pendency of the case is also critical, for it was reasonably foreseeable that the pending case would be before the newly elected justice. The fear of bias arises in such a situation when—without the other parties' consent—a man seems to choose the judge in his own cause. Applying this principle to the judicial election process, there was here a serious, objective risk of actual bias that required Justice Benjamin's recusal. In other words, on these extreme facts, the probability of actual bias rises to an unconstitutional level. Massey (D) is mistaken in predicting that this decision will lead to adverse consequences ranging from a flood of recusal motions to unnecessary interference with judicial elections. The case at bar presents an extraordinary situation whose circumstances are extreme by any measure, and, because the states may have codes of conduct with more rigorous recusal standards than due process requires, most recusal disputes will be resolved without resort to the Constitution, making the constitutional standard's application rare. Reversed and remanded.

DISSENT: (Roberts, C.J.) The majority's decision will undermine—not promote—impartiality on the bench. The majority's "probability of bias" standard is too undefined to provide adequate guidance as to when recusal is constitutionally mandated, which will inevitably lead to an increase in allegations that judges are biased, however groundless those charges may be. Despite the majority's repeated emphasis on the need for an "objective" standard, the standard announced by the majority is too vague to be objective. Even if the majority is correct that the case at bar is extreme, it does not follow that claims of judicial bias will not be brought to test the "probability of bias" standard, since claims that have little chance of success are nonetheless frequently filed. Regardless of their merits, such claims will inevitably bring the accused judge, and the judicial system as a whole, into disrepute. Moreover, it is not at all clear that the case at bar is, in fact, an extreme case. Blankenship's contributions were overwhelmingly independent contributions over which Benjamin had no control, and there were many other indications that Benjamin's election had nothing to do with Blankenship's contributions, but rather was influenced by his opponent's gaffes, newspaper endorsements, and other factors (other than contributions) that normally affect elections.

DISSENT: (Scalia, J.) Instead of promoting the public's confidence in the judicial system, the majority's decision will have the opposite effect, since what above all else is eroding public confidence in the judicial system is the perception that litigation is just a game to be won by the most resourceful lawyers. The majority's decision, through its indefiniteness, will reinforce that perception, by engendering vast uncertainty and enabling endless litigation of nonrecusal decisions.

ANALYSIS

In *Caperton*, the court seemingly rejected the well-established appearances-based recusal standard in favor of a probability-based standard that examines the likelihood of actual bias. The appearances-based standard is employed by the federal recusal statutes as well as state judicial codes of conduct, and the issue before the court was whether appearance of bias alone can rise to the level of a due process violation. Some courts—and Justice Benjamin himself—have taken

Continued on next page.

the position that due process does not require recusal based on the appearance of bias alone, and that due process is implicated only where actual bias is shown. Others have taken the position that mere appearance of bias can violate due process, and some take the position that "appearance of bias" and "probability of bias" are synonymous. By adopting the "probability of bias" standard, the majority arguably was aiming to avoid constitutionalizing the appearances-of-bias standard and to create an objective test based on the likelihood that a reasonable judge would actually be biased under a particular set of circumstances.

Quicknotes

BIAS Predisposition; preconception; refers to the tendency of a judge to favor or disfavor a particular party.

DUE PROCESS The constitutional mandate requiring the courts to protect and enforce individuals' rights and liberties consistent with prevailing principles of fairness and justice and prohibiting the federal and state governments from such activities that deprive its citizens of life, liberty, or property interest.

RECUSAL Procedure whereby a judge is disqualified from hearing a case either on his own behalf, or on the objection of a party, due to some bias or interest on the part of the judge in the subject matter of the suit.

CHAPTER 12

Control of Quality: Reducing the Likelihood of Professional Failure

Quick Reference Rules of Law

In re Glass

Bar applicant (P)

Cal. Sup. Ct., 316 P.3d 1199 (2014)

NATURE OF CASE: Review of bar application.

FACT SUMMARY: Stephen Randall Glass (P), a journalist made infamous by his fabricated stories, sources, and backgrounds, applied to the New York bar but withdrew when his moral character application was to be denied. He later applied to the California bar.

RULE OF LAW

An applicant cannot be accepted into a state bar if the applicant commits ongoing acts or crimes involving moral turpitude.

FACTS: Stephen Randall Glass (P) was a journalist with *The New Republic* magazine. During his tenure, he fabricated more than 40 articles with many of the articles focused on denigrating ethnic and racial minority groups. Glass (P) lied about sources, settings, and quotes. He fabricated background and supporting material so the fact checkers at *The New Republic* would not catch him in his lies. Over time, his editor, Charles Lane, became suspicious and confronted Glass (P) about one of his stories. After confirming it was false and facing those who continued to support Glass (P), Lane fired Glass (P) and the truth came out. Glass (P) had attended law school during this time and applied to the New York bar. He did not detail each of his falsehoods and did not accept complete responsibility. His moral character application was to be denied, so he withdrew it. Two years later, he applied to the California bar and was more detailed about his transgressions. [His bar application progressed to a hearing at the state bar court.]

ISSUE: Can an applicant be accepted into a state bar if the applicant commits ongoing acts or crimes involving moral turpitude?

HOLDING AND DECISION: (Per curiam) No. An applicant cannot be accepted into a state bar if the applicant commits ongoing acts or crimes involving moral turpitude. The protection of clients and the judicial system necessitates a lawyer's strong moral character. Glass (P) engaged in a campaign of unremitting journalistic dishonesty over a period of years. He violated journalism's Code of Ethics and even has been embodied in a museum as one of the worst journalistic deceivers. It is reprehensible this conduct occurred while he studied law and sought a license to practice law. He harmed the public and his profession when he fabricated material for his articles. He could so much more harm his clients and the legal profession if he falsified evidence. His many character witnesses attest to his rehabilitation but compassion for him is not the standard for this court. It is the court's duty to protect the public and maintain the integrity of the profession. Application denied.

ANALYSIS

The state bar character application requires a recitation of every lapse in judgment a prospective attorney may have experienced. Most states are lenient as to the occasional traffic violation or a one-time failure, but repeated unethical behavior and a refusal to take responsibility does not bode well for an applicant.

Quicknotes

MORAL TURPITUDE Intentional conduct demonstrating depravity or vileness and which is contrary to acceptable and traditional societal behavior.

Leis v. Flynt

Ohio judges (D) v. Magazine publisher (P)

439 U.S. 438 (1979)

NATURE OF CASE: Review of order enjoining criminal prosecution.

FACT SUMMARY: Out-of-state counsel for Flynt (P) contended that a state court's summary denial of their request to appear pro hac vice was unconstitutional.

RULE OF LAW

Absent a governing rule or statute, a summary denial of a request to appear pro hac vice is not unconstitutional.

FACTS: Flynt (P) was charged in an Ohio state court with various criminal acts in connection with distribution of his Hustler magazine. Flynt (P) retained Fahringer and Cambria as counsel, neither of whom were admitted to practice in Ohio. They requested admission pro hac vice. Ohio had no governing law or rule regarding pro hac vice admission. The trial court summarily denied the request, and the Ohio Supreme Court denied mandamus. Flynt (P) filed an action in federal district court, contending that the summary denial was unconstitutional and requesting that prosecution be enjoined. The district court enjoined the prosecution until such time as the trial court held a hearing based on clear legal standards. The Sixth Circuit Court of Appeals affirmed, and the United States Supreme Court granted certiorari.

ISSUE: Is a summary denial of a request to appear pro hac vice unconstitutional absent a governing rule or statute?

HOLDING AND DECISION: (Per curiam) No. Absent a governing rule or statute, a summary denial of a request to appear pro hac vice is not unconstitutional. The Constitution does not create property interests; rather, it guarantees due process protection to rights created elsewhere. In the context of this case, the right to practice pro hac vice cannot be created by the Constitution; such right must arise elsewhere. In Ohio, there is no law or rule governing pro hac vice admissions. Consequently, there is no source of a substantive right to practice that the Constitution might protect. This being so Flynt's (P) due process argument with respect to pro hac vice admission fails. Reversed.

DISSENT: (Stevens, J.) An attorney has a property interest in pursuing his calling. A state may not arbitrarily deny an out-of-state attorney the right to practice law in its courts. The denial of Flynt's (P) counsels' request bore no rational relationship to the goal of guaranteeing professional competence.

ANALYSIS

Pro hac vice admissions are becoming more and more commonplace. This is a reflection of several trends in the law. Increasing specialization has led to the demand for specialists to practice across state lines. Also, the trend toward "megafirms" which practice in many jurisdictions has tended to promote lawyer mobility.

Quicknotes

DUE PROCESS The constitutional mandate requiring the courts to protect and enforce individuals' rights and liberties consistent with prevailing principles of fairness and justice and prohibiting the federal and state governments from such activities that deprive its citizens of a life, liberty, or property interest.

PRO HAC VICE Applicable to a specific occasion; the use or application of a condition for the limited duration of a single situation.

Birbrower, Montalbano, Condon & Frank, P.C. v. Superior Court

Law firm (D/Petitioner), unlicensed in California, v. Court (Respondent); Corporation (P/Real Party in Interest)

Cal. Sup. Ct., 949 P.2d 1, *cert. denied*, 525 U.S. 920 (1998)

NATURE OF CASE: Appeal from judgment that law firm practiced law without a license and was therefore not entitled to collect under fee agreement.

FACT SUMMARY: Birbrower, Montalbano, Condon & Frank, P.C. (Birbrower) (D/Petitioner), a New York law firm unlicensed to practice law in California, performed legal services for ESQ Business Services, Inc. (ESQ) (P/Real Party in Interest), a California-based corporation, without a license. ESQ (P) refused to pay, alleging malpractice and claiming that the firm could not collect its fee because of its unauthorized practice of law. Birbrower (D) counterclaimed for its fee.

RULE OF LAW

Advising a client and negotiating a settlement agreement in California without a license constitutes the unauthorized practice of law for which no fee may be collected to the extent that the fee was for those services.

FACTS: ESQ Business Services, Inc. (ESQ) (P/Real Party in Interest), a California corporation, retained Birbrower, Montalbano, Condon & Frank, P.C. (Birbrower) (D/Petitioner), a New York law firm. None of the firm's attorneys were licensed to practice law in California. The fee agreement was negotiated and executed in New York, but provided that California law would govern all matters related to the representation. During several trips to California, the Birbrower (D) attorneys met with ESQ (P) and its accountants, gave legal advice, and made recommendations. They also spoke on their client's behalf during settlement agreement negotiations. ESQ (P) alleged malpractice, and Birbrower (D), counterclaimed to recover its fee.

ISSUE: Does advising a client and negotiating a settlement agreement in California without a license constitute the unauthorized practice of law for which no fee may be collected to the extent that the fee was for those services?

HOLDING AND DECISION: (Chin, J.) Yes. Advising a client and negotiating a settlement agreement in California without a license constitutes the unauthorized practice of law for which no fee may be collected to the extent that the fee was for those services. The court noted that the legal definition of "practicing law" included the giving of legal advice and the preparation of legal documents. The court then turned to the question of the meaning of "in California," holding that an unlicensed lawyer must engage in quantitatively sufficient activities within California or create a continuing attorney-client relationship for it to be determined that the attorney "practiced law in California." Although physical presence within the state is a factor, the court did not include that as a requirement in its analysis. Ruling that Birbrower's (D) actions constituted the extensive practice of law in California, the court declined to permit the firm from collecting its fee to the extent that the fee was based on any of the work it performed while in California. Affirmed in part, reversed in part, and remanded.

DISSENT: (Kennard, J.) This judge would define "practicing law" in a narrower way than the majority: "the representation of another in a judicial proceeding or an activity requiring the application of that degree of legal knowledge and technique possessed only by a trained legal mind." Because Birbrower's (D) activities while in California related only to arbitration, and arbitration is not necessarily "practicing law" under the above definition, the firm may have been entitled to relief.

ANALYSIS

The court recognized the distinction between the out-of-state litigator who obtains permission from a California judge to appear before that court pro hac vice and the out-of-state nonlitigator who cannot obtain similar authority to draft a legal document or provide legal advice to a client. Because case law offered no remedy for the nonlitigator who does not appear in a courtroom, the California legislature subsequently passed a law that permits, in effect, arbitrators the authority to admit out-of-state lawyers pro hac vice for in-state arbitrations.

Quicknotes

PRO HAC VICE Applicable to a specific occasion; the use or application of a condition for the limited duration of a single situation.

Linder v. Insurance Claims Consultants, Inc.

Insurance claimants (P) v. Insurance claim adjuster company (D)

S.C. Sup. Ct., 560 S.E.2d 612 (2002)

NATURE OF CASE: Action to declare contract void.

FACT SUMMARY: The Linders (P) contracted with Insurance Claims Consultants, Inc. (ICC) (D) for insurance adjustment services after property loss in a fire. ICC negotiated with the Linders' (P) insurance company about disputed claim payments and advised the Linders (P) about their coverage.

RULE OF LAW

Public insurance adjusters are not per se engaged in the unauthorized practice of law, but they may not engage in enumerated activities that require legal skill and knowledge.

FACTS: The Linders (P) suffered property damage in a fire. Their insurer did not approve their claim for full coverage of Mr. Linder's (P) gun collection. The Linders (P) contracted with Insurance Claims Consultants, Inc. (ICC) (D) to adjust their claims and agreed to pay ICC 10 percent of the total amount adjusted or recovered. ICC (D) advised the Linders (P) about their insurance coverage and policy language related to the gun collection and other claims. ICC (D) also engaged in negotiations with the insurer about claims. ICC (D) did get an increase of $12,000 claim payment to the Linders (P). The insurer delayed payment and the Linders (P), on advice of ICC (D), eventually retained counsel and then settled with the insurer. The Linders (P) refused to pay the 10 percent to ICC (D), so ICC (D) filed suit. The Linders (P) filed the instant action to declare the contract void because ICC (D) allegedly engaged in the unauthorized practice of law.

ISSUE: Are public insurance adjusters per se engaged in the unauthorized practice of law, and may they engage in activities that require legal skill and knowledge?

HOLDING AND DECISION: (Waller, J.) No. Public insurance adjusters are not per se engaged in the unauthorized practice of law, but they may not engage in enumerated activities that require legal skill and knowledge. This court has exclusive jurisdiction to define the practice of law in South Carolina. The purpose of regulating the legal profession is not to economically benefit lawyers but to protect the public from the consequences of actions or advice of people untrained in the law. The line between the authorized practice of law and the permissible business activities of non-lawyers may be unclear. South Carolina has not previously examined whether the business activities of insurance adjusters constitute the unauthorized practice of law. [The court examined other states' decisions.] While the business of public insurance adjusting does not per se constitute the practice of law, certain activities in which adjusters may engage do constitute the practice of law. An adjuster can assess value, discuss that value, and engage in negotiations about value with the client and the insurer. None of that requires legal skill or expertise. Permissible insurance adjuster practices include estimating damage and repair costs, preparing inventories on proof of loss, presenting claims to insurers, and negotiating property-damage valuations. Prohibited activities include advising clients on interpretations of the policy language, advising clients on whether to accept settlement offers from an insurer, becoming involved in coverage disputes, or advertising the provision of services requiring legal skill. Here, ICC (D) did advise the Linders (P) on their rights under their policy and became involved in the coverage dispute over Mr. Linder's (P) gun collection. ICC (D) thus did engage in the unauthorized practice of law. Much of ICC's (D) work did not entail the practice of law, so it is entitled to recover for the value of that work. ICC (D) may not be compensated for any unauthorized activities and that is the appropriate sanction for its unauthorized practice of law.

DISSENT: (Pleicones, J.) Licensed public adjusters should be permitted to interpret insurance contracts, negotiate coverage disputes, and advise clients on whether to accept settlement offers. Adjusters have particular expertise in these areas and clients hire them for their specialized knowledge. The Linders (P) hired ICC (D) for its knowledge that the gun collection should be covered and ICC (D) should not be prohibited from advising when it knows of a coverage issue. Public insurance adjusters, however, should refrain from advising the client once attorneys or the legal system becomes involved in the matter.

ANALYSIS

The "practice of law" is a fluid concept, but each state's highest court has the authority to determine what constitutes the practice of law as a matter of law within the state's borders. Some states are more restrictive with business practitioners than others when the practice veers too closely to legal advice. Businesses with specialized knowledge and skills may feel more qualified to advise clients in their area of expertise, but the consequences of poor advice can be severe. State supreme courts seek to protect the public from those consequences when they regulate the advice and services non-attorneys can provide.

CHAPTER 13

Control of Quality: Remedies for Professional Failure

Quick Reference Rules of Law

Togstad v. Vesely, Otto, Miller & Keefe

Paralysis victim (P) v. Law firm (D)

Minn. Sup. Ct., 291 N.W.2d 686 (1980)

NATURE OF CASE: Appeal of award of damages for legal malpractice.

FACT SUMMARY: Ms. Togstad (P) successfully sued Miller (D) of Vesely, Otto, Miller & Keefe (D) for legal malpractice, even though she had not formally retained him.

RULE OF LAW

A retainer is not required for an attorney-client relationship that may give rise to a malpractice claim to exist.

FACTS: Ms. Togstad (P) was rendered paralyzed after a medical procedure. Fourteen months later, Ms. Togstad (P) consulted with Miller (D) of Vesely, Otto, Miller & Keefe (D) regarding a possible malpractice action. After an initial consultation, Miller (D) informed Ms. Togstad (P) that he did not think she had a case, but that he would talk to his partners. Miller (D) never called back. After Minnesota's two-year statute of limitations on medical malpractice had expired, the Togstads (P) brought a legal malpractice action against Miller (D) for giving them erroneous advice and not advising them of the two-year statute. A jury found Miller (D) to have committed malpractice and awarded over $600,000 in damages. Miller (D) and his firm (D) appealed.

ISSUE: Is a retainer required for an attorney-client relationship that may give rise to a malpractice claim to exist?

HOLDING AND DECISION: (Per curiam) No. A retainer is not required for an attorney-client relationship that may give rise to a malpractice claim to exist. The first element in a malpractice claim is the existence of an attorney-client relationship. The crux of this relationship is the provision of advice by the attorney that he either knows or should know will be followed by the person to whom he provides the advice. This does not require actual retention. Here, Ms. Togstad (P) sought and obtained legal advice from Miller (D). It was entirely reasonable for Miller (D) to have expected the Togstads (P) to have followed his advice, which is exactly what they did. As a result, for purposes of a malpractice action, an attorney-client relationship between the Togstads (P) and Miller (D) existed. Affirmed.

ANALYSIS

It is unclear as to whether the attorney-client relationship is defined by contract or tort theory. Appellate courts around the nation have gone both ways on this issue, on a variety of grounds. The court here recognized this diversity of opinion but did not indicate its preference for the one theory over the other. The court believed the contract and tort analyses for this case to be so similar that they did not need to be distinguished.

Quicknotes

RETAINER Compensation paid in advance for professional services.

Smith v. Haynsworth, Marion, McKay & Geurard

Real estate developer (P) v. Law firm (D)

S.C. Sup. Ct., 472 S.E.2d 612 (1996)

NATURE OF CASE: Appeal from defense verdict in malpractice action.

FACT SUMMARY: In a malpractice action against the legal firm Haynsworth, Marion, McKay & Geurard (D), the court excluded from evidence proffered testimony regarding violations of the state's Rules of Professional Conduct by the attorneys (D).

RULE OF LAW

Rules of Professional Conduct may be relevant in establishing legal malpractice.

FACTS: Smith (P) sued the firm Haynsworth, Marion, McKay & Geurard (D) over the latter's representation of him in a land development scheme that went sour. At trial, Smith (P) sought to introduce evidence that the firm (D) had violated state Rules of Professional Conduct. The court excluded this evidence. The jury returned a verdict in favor of Haynsworth, Marion, McKay & Geurard (D), and Smith (P) appealed.

ISSUE: May Rules of Professional Conduct be relevant in establishing legal malpractice?

HOLDING AND DECISION: (Waller, J.) Yes. Rules of Professional Conduct may be relevant in establishing legal malpractice. A plaintiff in a malpractice action must establish the standard of care that he alleges the attorney-defendant violated, and this must be done through expert testimony. Such an expert, generally an attorney or law professor, may rely on Rules of Professional Conduct as a standard by which to gauge the defendant's standard of conduct, so long as the rule whose violation is alleged was intended to protect a person in the position of the plaintiff. Here, the proffered testimony would appear to fall within this standard, so it should have been allowed. Reversed and remanded.

ANALYSIS

States vary widely as to the extent to which they allow the use of rules of professional conduct to be used as a standard in malpractice actions. Some exclude them entirely, concluding that they are more prejudicial than probative. Others make their violation malpractice per se. The approach taken here could be described as a middle course between these two positions.

Quicknotes

EXPERT TESTIMONY Testimonial evidence about a complex area of subject matter relevant to trial, presented by a person competent to inform the trier of fact due to specialized knowledge or training.

LOCALITY A defined geographic region; the circumscribed location that defines the reach of a court's authority.

Viner v. Sweet

Clients of attorney (P) v. Attorney (D)

Cal. Sup. Ct., 70 P.3d 1046 (2003)

NATURE OF CASE: Appeal from a damages award.

FACT SUMMARY: When the Viners (P) brought a malpractice action against their attorney, Sweet (D), for failure to properly prepare legal documents that would have protected the Viners (P), Sweet (D) argued that the plaintiff, in order to prevail in a transactional legal malpractice action, must prove that a more favorable result would have been obtained but for the alleged negligence.

RULE OF LAW

The plaintiff in a transactional legal malpractice action must prove that a more favorable result would have been obtained but for the alleged negligence.

FACTS: Michael and Deborah Viner (P) retained attorney Sweet (D) to draft various legal instruments in regard to their company, such as a securities purchase agreement and an employment termination agreement, which contained a noncompetition provision. In fact, the contracts failed to provide a variety of safeguards, which Sweet (D) had led the Viners (P) to believe were provided. Subsequently, disputes arose between the Viners (P) and companies with which they had contracted. Because the agreements failed to provide the protections that Sweet (D) had said were provided to the Viners (P), the Viners (P) alleged a large loss of income and consequently brought a malpractice action against Sweet (D). The jury awarded damages. The court of appeals reduced the damages award, but otherwise affirmed the judgment, stating that the "but for" test was inappropriate in a transactional legal malpractice action. Sweet (D) appealed, arguing that there is nothing distinctive about transactional malpractice to justify a relaxation of, or departure from, the well-established requirement in negligence cases that causation be established by the "but for" test.

ISSUE: Must the plaintiff in a transactional legal malpractice action prove that a more favorable result would have been obtained but for the alleged negligence?

HOLDING AND DECISION: (Kennard, J.) Yes. The plaintiff in a transactional legal malpractice action must prove that a more favorable result would have been obtained but for the alleged negligence. There is nothing distinctive about transactional malpractice to justify a relaxation of, or departure from, the well-established requirement in negligence cases that causation be established by the "but for" test. When a business transaction goes awry, a natural target of the disappointed principals is the attorneys who arranged or advised the deal. Clients predictably attempt to shift some part of the loss and disappointment of a deal that goes sour onto the shoulders of persons who were responsible for the underlying legal work. Before the loss can be shifted, however, the client has an initial hurdle to clear. It must be shown that the loss suffered was in fact caused by the alleged attorney malpractice. It is far too easy to make the legal advisor a scapegoat for a variety of business misjudgments unless the courts pay close attention to the cause in fact element and deny recovery where the unfavorable outcome was likely to occur anyway, where the client already knew the problems with the deal, or where the client's own misconduct or misjudgment caused the problems. It is the failure of the client to establish the causal link that explains decisions where the loss is termed remote or speculative. Courts are properly cautious about making attorneys guarantors of their clients' faulty business judgment. We do not agree with the court of appeals that litigation is inherently or necessarily less complex than transactional work. Some litigation, such as many lawsuits involving car accidents, is relatively uncomplicated, but so too is much transactional work, such as the negotiation of a simple lease or a purchase and sale agreement. But some litigation, such as a beneficiary's action against a trustee challenging the trustee's management of trust property over a period of decades, is as complex as most transactional work. Furthermore, an attorney's representation of a client often combines litigation and transactional work, as when the attorney effects a settlement of pending litigation. Reversed.

ANALYSIS

As the California Supreme Court points out in the *Viner* decision, the purpose of the "but for" requirement, which has been in use for more than 120 years, is to safeguard against speculative and conjectural claims. It serves the essential purpose of ensuring that damages awarded for the attorney's malpractice "actually have been caused by the malpractice."

Continued on next page.

Quicknotes

"BUT FOR" TEST For purposes of determining tort liability, the test for the element of causation is whether the plaintiff would not have suffered the injury "but for" the defendant's conduct.

FIDUCIARY DUTY A legal obligation to act for the benefit of another, including subordinating one's personal interests to that of the other person.

PROFESSIONAL NEGLIGENCE The breach of a fiduciary duty owed to one's client, caused by the professional's actions and injurious to the client.

In re Jordan Schiff

[N/A]

Departmental Disciplinary Committee, N.Y. Sup. Ct., Docket No. HP 22/92 (1993)

NATURE OF CASE: Disciplinary action taken in response to allegations of misconduct by an attorney during a deposition.

FACT SUMMARY: This disciplinary hearing was held after Schiff (D) allegedly violated the code of ethics by using obscene, explicit, gender-specific vulgarities to harass opposing female counsel during a deposition.

RULE OF LAW

Attorneys who direct dirty, discriminatory, gutter language at opposing counsel to harass counsel on the basis of gender will be subject to sanction for violation of the rules of professional ethics.

FACTS: During a deposition of a client which his firm represented in a personal injury suit, Schiff (D) used obscene, explicit, gender-specific vulgarities in an attempt to intimidate and harass opposing counsel, Mark (P). Early in the deposition, a senior partner of Schiff's (D) firm had set the tone by standing and shouting at Mark (P). During a hearing held by the Disciplinary Committee, both the court reporter and the Spanish interpreter testified that, off the record, Schiff (D) referred to Mark (P) as a "cunt" and an "asshole" and said she should "go home and have babies." On the record, the deposition itself was replete with sexual obscenities uttered by Schiff (D).

ISSUE: Will attorneys who direct dirty, discriminatory, gutter language at opposing counsel to harass counsel on the basis of gender be subject to sanction for violation of the rules of professional ethics?

HOLDING AND DECISION: (Elsen, Panel Chair) Yes. Attorneys who direct dirty, discriminatory, gutter language at opposing counsel to harass counsel on the basis of gender will be subject to sanction for violation of the rules of professional ethics. In mitigation, Schiff (D) apologized to Mark (P) by letter and at the hearing. However, the record shows that the apology and sanctions imposed on Schiff's (D) law firm were insufficient to convince him that his conduct was in need of reform. Evidence of a later deposition in another case reveals Schiff (D) used gender-specific vulgarities again in speaking to opposing female counsel. On the evidence presented, all charges against Schiff (D) of ethics violations are sustained. The sanction will be public censure.

ANALYSIS

The panel declared that were it not for Schiff's (D) unblemished record and his youth, plus the consideration that he was no longer with the firm that set him such a bad example, their recommendation would be even more severe. Public censure was deemed appropriate because those in the profession must understand that sexual harassment is unacceptable, and the public must understand that the profession abhors such behavior and will not condone it. In censuring Schiff (D), *In Re Schiff*, 190 A.D.2d 293 (1993), the court described his conduct as "inexcusable and intolerable, reflecting adversely on his fitness to practice law."

Quicknotes

PUBLIC CENSURE A statement issued by a governing body toward one of its members officially reprimanding that person, and carrying a higher degree of professional disgrace than a simple reprimand because it is made public.

CHAPTER 14

Control of Quality: Nonlawyers in the Law Business (and Related Issues)

Quick Reference Rules of Law

NAACP v. Button

Political organization (P) v. State official (D)

371 U.S. 415 (1963)

NATURE OF CASE: Review of order rejecting constitutional challenge to anti-solicitation law.

FACT SUMMARY: Virginia (D) enacted a law prohibiting the solicitation of clients by an agent of an organization or individual that retained a lawyer in connection with an action in which it was neither a party nor had a pecuniary interest.

RULE OF LAW

A state may not constitutionally prohibit the solicitation of clients by an agent of an individual or organization that retains a lawyer in connection with an action in which it is neither a party nor has a pecuniary interest.

FACTS: The Virginia Chapter of the National Association for the Advancement of Colored People (the NAACP) (P) had for years engaged in the activity of locating (soliciting) potential plaintiffs to be litigants in suits aimed at fulfilling the NAACP's (P) political objectives of ending segregation. In response, the state of Virginia (D) enacted an anti-solicitation law prohibiting the agent of an organization or individual from soliciting clients for lawsuits in which the organization or individual paid for the lawyer in connection with an action in which the organization or individual was neither a party nor had a pecuniary interest. Because the attorneys to whom the NAACP (P) would refer potential litigants were usually on the NAACP (P) staff, this effectively prohibited the NAACP's (P) solicitation procedure. The NAACP (P) challenged this as violative of the First Amendment. The state's highest court rejected this contention, and the United States Supreme Court granted certiorari.

ISSUE: May a state constitutionally prohibit the solicitation of clients by an agent of an individual or organization that retains a lawyer in connection with an action in which it is neither a party nor has a pecuniary interest?

HOLDING AND DECISION: (Brennan, J.) No. A state may not constitutionally prohibit the solicitation of clients by an agent of an individual or organization that retains a lawyer in connection with an action in which it is neither a party nor has a pecuniary interest. Solicitation is covered by the First Amendment, since abstract discussion is not the only species of communication protected by the First Amendment; vigorous advocacy is protected by it as well. Litigation is more than a vehicle for resolving private disputes; it is a means for achieving lawful political ends, and in that regard it is political expression. Under the conditions of government, litigation is sometimes the only practicable way an unpopular group can petition for redress of grievances. The First Amendment protects certain forms of group activity, and using litigation to achieve political ends is one such form of activity. That is, association for litigation is a form of political association. Under the statute at issue, a person who advises another that his legal rights have been infringed and refers him to a particular attorney or group of attorneys for assistance has committed a crime, as has the attorney who knowingly renders assistance under such circumstances; the statute thus poses the grave danger of unconstitutionally eliminating any discussion relating to the institution of litigation on behalf of unpopular minorities. Since the use of litigation is a constitutionally protected activity, Virginia (D) must show a compelling reason for its existence. The proffered justification is the state interest in regulating the legal profession and against solicitation and barratry. While these are important objectives, the type of solicitation at issue here differs materially from solicitation of a for-profit nature, which a state may well be able to prohibit. Such is not at issue here. Since a compelling reason for the prohibition has not been shown, it is constitutionally defective. Reversed.

DISSENT: (Harlan, J.) An attorney retained by the NAACP (P) to promote its causes—ordinarily an NAACP (P) staff attorney—does not form a normal attorney-client relationship with his "client." The form of pleading, the relief requested, and the timing of lawsuits are all decided by the NAACP (P), not the attorney, to whom he is essentially beholden. Virginia (D) has an interest in maintaining high professional standards in its legal profession. It has never been seriously disputed that laws against solicitation and barratry are valid, and the law at issue finds its roots therein. The majority distinguishes the statute from other types of regulation of solicitation and barratry by noting that the type of suits the NAACP (P) initiates are not of the for-profit nature. This is a too-facile analysis, since the avoidance of pecuniary gain is not the only relevant factor in determining appropriate standards of lawyer conduct. A lawyer in the type of actions maintained by the NAACP (P) finds himself in a divided allegiance. A state has an interest in preventing attorney conflicts of interest, and this legitimizes the law in question. Moreover, the statute here does not

Continued on next page.

unreasonably impede the assertion of federal rights and is consistent with federal standing rules.

ANALYSIS

Ethical Consideration 5-1 of Canon 5 of the ABA Code of Professional Responsibility provides: "The professional judgment of a lawyer should be exercised, within the bounds of the law, solely for the benefit of his client and free of compromising influences and loyalties. Neither his personal interests, the interests of other clients, nor the desires of third persons should be permitted to dilute his loyalty to his client." An attorney retained by an organization which has solicited litigants to further its political ends through litigation will almost certainly have to deal with this consideration at some point, and may at some point face a conflict of interest that will require the attorney's withdrawal.

Quicknotes

BARRATRY The practice of generating lawsuits. Most jurisdictions consider it a crime.

CONFLICT OF INTEREST Ethical problems that arise, or may be anticipated to arise, between an attorney and the client if the interests of the attorney, another client, or a third party conflict with those of the present client.

RETAINER Compensation paid in advance for professional services.

Continued on next page.

In re Primus

[N/A]

436 U.S. 412 (1978)

NATURE OF CASE: Review of attorney reprimand.

FACT SUMMARY: The South Carolina Bar reprimanded Primus for forwarding a letter to an individual advising her of certain rights and of the opportunity to receive free legal services.

RULE OF LAW

A state may not prohibit attorneys from mailing letters to potential clients advising them of their legal rights and of the opportunity to receive free legal services.

FACTS: Primus, an attorney, in conjunction with the American Civil Liberties Union (ACLU), forwarded a letter to one Williams, who had been sterilized as part of a state regulatory practice conditioning entitlement to welfare payments on sterilization. The letter advised Williams that she had a potential claim against the doctor who performed the procedure, and that the ACLU had a legal staff that could perform free legal services for her. Williams declined to pursue the matter, but the state bar, under a disciplinary rule prohibiting solicitation by letter, published a letter of reprimand against Primus. The South Carolina Supreme Court affirmed the reprimand, and the United States Supreme Court granted review.

ISSUE: May a state prohibit attorneys from mailing letters to potential clients advising them of their legal rights and of the opportunity to receive free legal services?

HOLDING AND DECISION: (Powell, J.) No. A state may not prohibit attorneys from mailing letters to potential clients advising them of their legal rights and of the opportunity to receive free legal services. When legal services are performed as part of an attempt to further a political agenda, such activities constitute a form of expression protected under the First and Fourteenth Amendments. State abridgements on such activities must be narrowly tailored to serve a compelling interest. Here, there can be little question but that Primus's solicitation was part of an effort to advance a political program; the ACLU is well known for taking political positions, and the fact that it might benefit at some later date because of a regulated lawsuit does not alter this. Consequently, Primus's letter was a form of protected expression. The proffered state interest is the prevention of overreaching and intimidation of potential clients. While a state has a compelling interest in prohibiting this behavior, it has not been shown that a blanket prohibition on solicitation by mail is necessary to achieve this end. Since the state prohibition is not narrowly drawn, it is unconstitutional. Reversed.

ANALYSIS

This case was decided the same day as *Ohralik v. Ohio State Bar Assn.*, 436 U.S. 447 (1978). These two cases appear to show the outer limits of a state's ability to prohibit attorney solicitation. It would seem the cases can be read to permit a state to prohibit completely all attorney in-person solicitation. All other solicitations, if politically motivated, must be reviewed on a case-by-case basis.

Quicknotes

COMMERCIAL SPEECH Any speech that proposes a commercial transaction or promotes products or services.

FREEDOM OF ASSOCIATION The right to peaceably assemble.

United Transportation Union v. State Bar of Michigan

Railworkers' union (D) v. Michigan state bar (P)

401 U.S. 576 (1971)

NATURE OF CASE: Review of order enjoining a labor union from procuring legal services for its members.

FACT SUMMARY: The Michigan State Bar (P) challenged the United Transportation Union's (D) practice of obtaining low-cost legal services for its members.

RULE OF LAW

A labor union can assist its members in obtaining low-cost legal services.

FACTS: The United Transportation Union (the Union) (D) instituted a program to assist its members who had causes of action under the Federal Employers' Liability Act. The Union (D) would refer its members to selected attorneys, who had agreed to charge a fee of no more than 25 percent of total recovery. The Michigan State Bar (P) challenged this practice as illegal "solicitation" of lawsuits. A state trial court enjoined the practice, and the Michigan Supreme Court affirmed. The United States Supreme Court granted review.

ISSUE: Can a labor union assist its members in obtaining low-cost legal services?

HOLDING AND DECISION: (Black, J.) Yes. A labor union can assist its members in obtaining low-cost legal services. This court has already held that the First Amendment permits groups to unite to assert their legal rights as effectively and economically as possible. An organization may also employ attorneys to represent its members. From this it follows that an organization may also refer its members to attorneys. The injunction at issue here not only prohibited the Union (D) from so doing, but also enjoined it from doing various acts incident thereto, such as providing information concerning the availability of legal service and compensating individuals for the time spent providing such information. If an organization is to be permitted to assert its legal rights, the activities enjoined in this particular case must also be permitted. Reversed.

ANALYSIS

The case principally relied upon by the court here was *NAACP v. Button*, 371 U.S. 415 (1963). A difference existed between the situation in *NAACP* and the present case, in that the prior action involved ideologically motivated litigation as opposed to the purely economic interests at issue here. It is not clear whether this distinction was raised, and based on the court's inclinations as evidenced by the language of the opinion, it is unlikely that it would have altered the holding.

Quicknotes

FIRST AMENDMENT Prohibits Congress from enacting any law respecting an establishment of religion or prohibiting the free exercise of religion; abridging freedom of speech or of the press; the right of peaceful assembly; and the right to petition for a redress of grievances.

Maslowski v. Prospect Funding Partners LLC

Seller of rights to litigation proceeds (P) v. Litigation finance company (D)

Minn. Sup. Ct., 944 N.W.2d 235 (2020)

NATURE OF CASE: [Appeal from affirmance of dismissal of defendant's counterclaim for breach of contract and unjust enrichment in declaratory judgment action seeking to avoid litigation financing agreement as champertous and against public policy.]

FACT SUMMARY: Pamela Maslowski (P) contended that the contract she entered into with Prospect Funding Partners LLC (Prospect) (D), whereby she sold to Prospect (D) an interest in a portion of any recovery she would get in her personal injury suit, was champertous and void as against public policy. Prospect (D) countered, claiming that the contract was enforceable and that when Maslowski (P), who prevailed in her personal injury suit, refused to pay Prospect (D), Maslowski (P) breached the contract and was unjustly enriched.

RULE OF LAW

A litigation finance agreement, whereby a plaintiff in a lawsuit sells to a litigation finance company an interest in a portion of any recovery the plaintiff obtains in the lawsuit, in exchange for an advance of a sum certain, is not champertous and violative of public policy.

FACTS: Pamela Maslowski (P) was the plaintiff in a personal injury action. Needing money for living expenses while her action was pending, she entered into a litigation financing agreement with Prospect Funding Partners LLC (Prospect) (D). Under the agreement, Maslowski (P) sold to Prospect (D) the right to receive a portion of the proceeds of any settlement that she received from her personal injury suit. As consideration for the sale, Maslowski (P) received $6,000 from Prospect (D) that was essentially a cash advance on her prospective settlement. Under the contract's fee schedule, the amount Maslowski (P) owed to Prospect (D) increased by 30 percent every six months, starting from a baseline of the $6,000 plus fees, with a cap at $25,245.00. However, if Maslowski (P) did not receive a settlement, she owed Prospect (D) nothing. The contract also provided that Maslowski's (P) obligation to Prospect (D) would not exceed the amount of her settlement. Maslowski's (P) attorney in the personal injury suit discussed the contract with her and signed the last page of the agreement certifying that he had reviewed the terms with Maslowski (P) and acknowledged the payment directions in the event of a settlement. On June 22, 2015, Prospect informed Maslowski she would owe Prospect $14,108.00 if her personal injury claim settled and she made payment to Prospect before September 22, 2015. Maslowski's attorney then informed Prospect that he believed that the litigation financing agreement between Maslowski and Prospect was unenforceable. The suit settled in July of 2015, but Maslowski (P) refused to pay Prospect (D). [Maslowski (P) brought a declaratory judgment action against Prospect (D), claiming that the agreement was champertous and against public policy. Prospect (D) counterclaimed, asserting claims for breach of contract and unjust enrichment. The trial court ruled that the agreement was "unenforceable and void" because it violated the state's common-law prohibition against champerty and maintenance. The state's intermediate appellate court affirmed, and the state's highest court granted review.]

ISSUE: Is a litigation finance agreement, whereby a plaintiff in a lawsuit sells to a litigation finance company an interest in a portion of any recovery the plaintiff obtains in the lawsuit, in exchange for an advance of a sum certain, champertous and violative of public policy?

HOLDING AND DECISION: (Hudson, J.) No. A litigation finance agreement, whereby a plaintiff in a lawsuit sells to a litigation finance company an interest in a portion of any recovery the plaintiff obtains in the lawsuit, in exchange for an advance of a sum certain, is not champertous and violative of public policy. Champerty is an agreement to divide litigation proceeds between the owner of the litigated claim and a party unrelated to the lawsuit who supports or helps enforce the claim. Pursuant to the state's common law, the contract between Maslowski (P) and Prospect (D) is champertous, and the lower courts did not err in determining that, under precedent, the contract was unenforceable. However, based on current public policy, societal values, and changes in the legal profession, the ancient prohibition against champerty is no longer necessary. First, rules of ethics and rules of civil procedure address the abuses of the legal process that necessitated the common-law prohibition. Second, although contingency fees were disfavored under early common law, all American jurisdictions now allow attorneys to take cases on contingency, and contingent fee agreements are viewed as a way to facilitate access to justice by incentivizing attorneys to take cases that they might otherwise decline because the client cannot afford their services on an hourly or fixed-fee basis; litigation financing agreements may likewise increase such access. Third, many in society now see a litigated claim as a potentially valuable asset, rather than viewing litigation as an evil to be avoided. Maslowski (P) argues that these

Continued on next page.

changes do not justify an abolition of the common-law prohibition against champerty. First, she contends that the rules of professional responsibility and civil procedure are insufficient because they do not regulate the substance of champertous agreements. Second, she argues that litigation financing agreements have the potential to strip tort victims of their recovery. Third, she claims that champertous agreements will deter plaintiffs from settling their claims because they will need larger settlements to offset the cost of litigation financing. Although it is true that the rules of professional responsibility and civil procedure do not specifically regulate champertous agreements, these rules prevent both attorneys and parties from profiting off of frivolous litigation—which is the type of behavior that the champerty prohibition was intended to prevent. It is also unlikely that companies like Prospect (D) will fund frivolous claims because they only profit from their investment if a plaintiff receives a settlement that exceeds the amount of the advance—an unlikely result in a meritless suit—and such companies have claim valuation procedures to avoid this very problem. Additionally, though it is important that the victims of torts receive compensation for their injuries, they nonetheless have the freedom to contract, and many parties to litigation finance agreements are sophisticated and understand the risks involved. Furthermore, Maslowski (P) presents no empirical evidence to support her argument that litigation financing "under-incentivizes settlement." Just as contingency fees are permitted because they allow plaintiffs who would otherwise be priced out of the justice system to assert their rights, the same is true of litigation financing. Finally, the courts serve as safeguards against inequitable litigation financing agreements, and the parties who sell interests in their litigation retain the defense of unconscionability. For these reasons, the state's common-law prohibition against champerty is abolished. [Reversed.]

ANALYSIS

The court in *Maslowski* estimated that the size of the litigation finance market, which is valued at $50 to $100 billion, reflects society's changed values about champerty. Because society has become increasingly litigious, businesses often seek financing to mitigate the risks associated with litigation and to maintain cash flow for their operations. Although the court abolished the prohibition against champerty, it admonished courts to carefully review uncounseled agreements, particularly between parties of unequal bargaining power or agreements involving an unsophisticated party. The court also admonished courts and attorneys to be careful to ensure that litigation financiers do not attempt to control the course of the underlying litigation, as such intermeddling was a significant concern of early champerty precedent.

Quicknotes

CHAMPERTY An agreement to divide litigation proceeds between the owner of a litigated claim and a party unrelated to the lawsuit who supports or helps enforce the claim.

LITIGATION FINANCE AGREEMENT A contract where a third party unrelated to a lawsuit provides capital to the lawsuit's plaintiff in exchange for an interest in a portion of any financial recovery the plaintiff may obtain in the litigation.

CHAPTER 15

Free Speech Rights of Lawyers and Judicial Candidates

Quick Reference Rules of Law

In re Holtzman

[N/A]

N.Y. Ct. App., 577 N.E.2d 30, *cert. denied*, 502 U.S. 1009 (1991)

NATURE OF CASE: Appeal of admonition for attorney conduct.

FACT SUMMARY: Holtzman (D), admonished for falsely accusing a judge of improper behavior, contended that such an admonition required a finding of constitutional malice.

RULE OF LAW

It is not necessary for an attorney to act with constitutional malice in order for the attorney to be disciplined for issuing false statements.

FACTS: Holtzman (D), the Kings County District Attorney, released a letter to the media alleging that a trial court judge behaved improperly. An investigation revealed that her accusations were false. She was then admonished under attorney disciplinary rules for the false accusations. She appealed the admonition, contending that state bar authorities had to find that she acted with constitutional malice in order to discipline her.

ISSUE: Is it necessary for an attorney to act with constitutional malice in order for the attorney to be disciplined for issuing false statements?

HOLDING AND DECISION: (Per curiam) No. It is not necessary for an attorney to act with constitutional malice in order for the attorney to be disciplined for issuing false statements. Unlike defamation, to which constitutional malice applies, professional responsibility is not an essentially private matter but rather is rendered for the benefit of the public at large. When an attorney makes a false statement, the issue is not whether a reputation has been harmed but rather whether the administration of justice has been hampered. To substitute objective analysis of this question with the subjective standard of constitutional malice would undercut the premise of professional responsibility, which would be against the public interest. Affirmed.

ANALYSIS

In the adversarial atmosphere of the courtroom, it is natural that attorneys and judges will lock horns. This sometimes results in public statements by attorneys about judges that are less than flattering. All states have limits on what attorneys can say about judges, limits which attorneys often cross to their regret.

Quicknotes

MALICE The intention to commit an unlawful act without justification or excuse.

NEW YORK CODE OF PROFESSIONAL RESPONSIBILITY DR 1-102(A)(6) A lawyer shall not engage in any other conduct that adversely reflects on his fitness to practice law.

Republican Party of Minnesota v. White

Political party (P) v. State judicial official (D)

536 U.S. 765 (2002)

NATURE OF CASE: Appeal from decision that a state's judiciary, without violating the First Amendment, may prohibit candidates for judicial election in that state from announcing their views on disputed legal or political issues.

FACT SUMMARY: The state's highest court adopted a canon of judicial conduct that prohibited a candidate for judicial office from "announc[ing] his or her views on disputed legal or political issues" (announce clause). While running for associate justice of that court, Wersal (and others) (P) filed suit seeking a declaration that the announce clause violated the First Amendment.

RULE OF LAW

The First Amendment prohibits a state's judiciary from prohibiting candidates for judicial election in that state from announcing their views on disputed legal and political issues.

FACTS: The state's highest court adopted a canon of judicial conduct that prohibited a "candidate for a judicial office" from "announc[ing] his or her views on disputed legal or political issues" (announce clause). Incumbent judges who violated this rule were subject to discipline, including removal, censure, civil penalties, and suspension without pay. Lawyers who ran for judicial office also had to comply with the announce clause. While running for associate justice of the state's highest court, Wersal (and others) (P) filed suit in federal district court seeking a declaration that the announce clause was violative of the First Amendment and an injunction against its enforcement. The district court held that the announce clause was constitutional and granted summary judgment to the state (D). The court of appeals affirmed, and the United States Supreme Court granted certiorari.

ISSUE: Does the First Amendment prohibit a state's judiciary from prohibiting candidates for judicial election in that state from announcing their views on disputed legal and political issues?

HOLDING AND DECISION: (Scalia, J.) Yes. The First Amendment prohibits a state's judiciary from prohibiting candidates for judicial election in that state from announcing their views on disputed legal and political issues. "Announcing views" on an issue covers much more than promising to decide an issue a certain way, and the announce clause prohibits a candidate's mere statements of his current position, even if he doesn't bind himself to maintain that position after election. Although the clause was construed in the courts below to reach only disputed issues that are likely to come before the candidate if he is elected, this limitation is not much of a limitation because there is almost no legal or political issue that is unlikely to come before a judge of an American court. The record demonstrates that the announce clause prohibits a judicial candidate from stating his views on any specific nonfanciful legal question within the province of the court for which he is running, except in the context of discussing past decisions—and in the latter context as well, if he expresses the view that he is not bound by stare decisis. The state (D) argues that this still leaves plenty of topics for discussion on the campaign trail, such as a candidate's character, education, work habits, etc., and, in fact, the state's (D) judicial board has published a list of preapproved questions that judicial candidates are allowed to answer. The issue then becomes whether these preapproved subjects fulfill the First Amendment's free speech guarantee. The announce clause both prohibits speech based on its content and burdens a category of speech that is at the core of First Amendment freedoms—speech about the qualifications of candidates for public office. The court of appeals concluded, and the parties do not dispute, that the proper test to be applied to determine the constitutionality of such a restriction is strict scrutiny, under which respondents have the burden to prove that the clause is (1) narrowly tailored, to serve (2) a compelling state interest. That court found that the state (D) had established two interests as sufficiently compelling to justify the announce clause: preserving the state judiciary's impartiality and preserving the appearance of that impartiality. Under any definition of "impartiality," the announce clause fails strict scrutiny. First, it is plain that the clause is not narrowly tailored to serve impartiality (or its appearance) in the traditional sense of the word, i.e., as a lack of bias for or against either party to the proceeding. Indeed, the clause is barely tailored to serve that interest at all, inasmuch as it does not restrict speech for or against particular parties, but rather speech for or against particular issues. If a party loses a case that turns on a legal issue the judge had taken a stand on as a candidate, it is not because of bias against the party, but because the judge is evenhandedly applying the law as he sees it—any party coming before the judge taking a position contrary to the judge's view would lose. Second, although "impartiality" in the sense of a lack of preconception in favor of or against a particular legal view may well be an interest served by the announce clause,

Continued on next page.

pursuing this objective is not a compelling state interest, since it is virtually impossible, and hardly desirable, to find a judge who does not have preconceptions about the law. In fact, the state's constitution positively forbids the selection to courts of judges who are impartial in the sense of having no views on the law because all judges must be learned in the law. Third, the court need not decide whether achieving "impartiality" (or its appearance) in the sense of openmindedness is a compelling state interest because, as a means of pursuing this interest, the announce clause is so woefully underinclusive that the court does not believe it was adopted for that purpose. This is demonstrated by the fact that statements made in an election campaign are an infinitesimal portion of the statements judges and judges-to-be make that commit them to a legal position, because they have committed themselves before coming to the bench or while on the bench. Such commitments have been made in prior rulings or in nonadjudicatory settings, such as in classes they conduct, books, and speeches. Thus, a candidate for judicial office may make such a commitment before he announces his candidacy or after he is elected. Justice Stevens asserts in his dissent that statements made in an election campaign pose a special threat to openmindedness because the candidate, when elected judge, will have a particular reluctance to contradict them. While this may be true with regard to campaign promises, promises are not at issue here because they are regulated separately. Also, with regard to nonpromissory commitments to a certain position, it is not self-evident that judges will find these more binding on them than a carefully considered holding. The state (D) has not carried the burden imposed by strict scrutiny of establishing that statements made during an election campaign are uniquely destructive of openmindedness. Justice Stevens is wrong in his broad assertion that to the extent statements on legal issues seek to enhance a candidate's popularity they evidence a lack of fitness for office. Such statements are made in all confirmation hearings, and thus Justice Stevens must think the entire federal bench is unfit. Moreover, the notion that the special context of electioneering justifies an abridgment of the right to speak out on disputed issues sets First Amendment jurisprudence on its head. We have never allowed the government to prohibit candidates from communicating relevant information to voters during an election, but Justice Ginsburg would do so. She contends that the announce clause must be constitutional because due process would be denied if an elected judge sat in a case involving an issue on which he had previously announced his view. She reaches this conclusion because, she says, such a judge would have a "direct, personal, substantial, and pecuniary interest" in ruling consistently with his previously announced view, in order to reduce the risk that he will be "voted off the bench and thereby lose his salary and emoluments," but elected judges—regardless of whether they have announced any views beforehand—always face the pressure of an electorate who might disagree with their rulings and therefore vote them off the bench. If it violates due process for a judge to sit in a case in which ruling one way rather than another increases his prospects for reelection, then by Justice Ginsburg's logic, the practice of electing judges is itself a violation of due process. Finally, although a universal and long-established tradition of prohibiting certain conduct creates a strong presumption the prohibition is constitutional, the practice of prohibiting speech by judicial candidates is neither ancient nor universal. The court knows of no such prohibitions throughout the 19th and the first quarter of the 20th century, and they are still not universally adopted. This does not compare well with the traditions deemed worthy of attention. There is an obvious tension between the state's constitution, which requires judicial elections, and the announce clause, which places most subjects of interest to the voters off limits. The First Amendment does not permit the state (D) to leave the principle of elections in place while preventing candidates from discussing what the elections are about. Reversed.

DISSENT: (Ginsburg, J.) Elections for political offices, in which the First Amendment holds full sway, must be distinguished from elections designed to select those whose office it is to administer justice without respect to persons. The state's (D) choice to elect its judges does not preclude the state (D) from installing an election process geared to the judicial office. As agents of the people, legislative and executive officials serve in representative capacities, and therefore, candidates for these representative offices must be left free to inform the electorate of their positions on specific issues. Judges, however, are not representatives of particular persons, communities, or parties; they serve no faction or constituency. They must strive to do what is legally right, even in the face of unpopularity. In addition, the majority ignores a crucial limiting construction placed on the announce clause by the courts below. The provision does not bar a candidate from generally stating views on legal questions; it only prevents her from publicly making known how she would decide disputed issues. That limitation places beyond the scope of the announce clause a wide range of comments that may be highly informative to voters, including statements of historical fact; qualified statements; and statements framed at a sufficient level of generality. The announce clause is thus narrower, and campaigns conducted under that provision more robust, than the majority's construction of the clause acknowledges. Judicial candidates may not only convey general information about themselves, but they may describe their conception of the role of a judge and their views on a wide range of subjects of interest to the voters. Further, they may discuss, criticize, or defend

Continued on next page.

past decisions of interest to voters. What they may not do is remove themselves from the constraints characteristic of the judicial office and declare how they would decide an issue, without regard to the particular context in which it is presented. Properly construed, the announce clause prohibits only a discrete subcategory of the statements the majority's misinterpretation encompasses. Moreover, the majority ignores the significance of the announce clause to the state's (D) judicial election system, and its interdependence with the state's (D) rule prohibiting candidates from making pledges or promises of conduct in office other than the faithful and impartial performance of the duties of the office. The pledge or promise rule promotes the public faith in the judiciary by attempting to eliminate the perception that a judge's ruling is merely a quid pro quo for being elected on a campaign promise. The state's (D) interest in the pledges or promises clause is thus significant, and its constitutionality supported. The announce clause is equally important to achieving these constitutional ends, since without it, the pledges or promises clause would be weak. That is because without the announce clause, the pledges and promises clause can be easily circumvented by a candidate who does not promise anything, but merely announces his or her position on a given issue. Both the promise and the statement contemplate a quid pro quo between the candidate and the voters, and, contrary to the majority's belief, the nonpromissory statement does nothing to avert the dangers inherent in the promissory statement. The announce clause prevents this circumvention of the pledges or promises clause, and, therefore is an indispensable— and constitutional— part of the state's (D) effort to maintain a healthy judiciary.

ANALYSIS

This decision presents the difficult issue of whether the restrictions on certain statements made by candidates for judicial office are impermissible content-based restrictions, or permissible content-based restrictions that survive strict scrutiny based on the government's strong interest in preserving judicial independence and impartiality (and the appearance thereof). Hence, the majority focuses on the content of the speech being regulated, whereas the dissent focuses on the government interest. In 2007, the ABA changed its Code of Judicial Conduct to satisfy the decision in this case by eliminating the announce clause and providing an expanded pledges or promises clause.

Quicknotes

CERTIORARI A discretionary writ issued by a superior court to an inferior court in order to review the lower court's decisions; the Supreme Court's writ ordering such review.

FIRST AMENDMENT Prohibits Congress from enacting any law respecting an establishment of religion or prohibiting the free exercise of religion; abridging freedom of speech or of the press; the right of peaceful assembly; and the right to petition for a redress of grievances.

INJUNCTION A court order requiring a person to do, or prohibiting that person from doing, a specific act.

STARE DECISIS Doctrine whereby courts follow legal precedent unless there is good cause for departure.

CHAPTER 16

Marketing Legal Services

Quick Reference Rules of Law

Ohralik v. Ohio State Bar Assn.

Attorney (D) v. Ohio state bar (P)

436 U.S. 447 (1978)

NATURE OF CASE: Review of order suspending attorney from practice.

FACT SUMMARY: Ohralik (D) solicited two young women who had been in a car accident, visiting one while she was in traction in the hospital.

RULE OF LAW

A state may constitutionally discipline a lawyer for soliciting clients in person, for pecuniary gain, under circumstances likely to pose dangers that the state has a right to prevent.

FACTS: Attorney Ohralik (D), upon learning about an auto accident involving an eighteen-year-old woman, twice visited her in the hospital, whereupon she orally agreed to allow him to represent her. She later sought to renege on the agreement. He also solicited as a client the woman's passenger. The Ohio State Bar (P) instituted disciplinary proceedings, alleging that Ohralik (D) had violated disciplinary rules barring in-person solicitation of clients. Ohralik (D) was indefinitely suspended. The United States Supreme Court granted review.

ISSUE: May a state constitutionally discipline a lawyer for soliciting clients in person, for pecuniary gain, under circumstances likely to pose dangers that the state has a right to prevent.?

HOLDING AND DECISION: (Powell, J.) Yes. A state may constitutionally discipline a lawyer for soliciting clients in person, for pecuniary gain, under circumstances likely to pose dangers that the state has a right to prevent. A state has a strong interest in preventing the perceived harms of attorney solicitation—these being assertion of fraudulent claims, debasement of the legal profession, and potential harm to the client by overreaching, overcharging, underrepresentation, and misrepresentation. The potential for coercion of the prospective client is particularly strong in a face-to-face solicitation, as the attorney, who is trained in persuasion, holds a great advantage over the client, who is at best unfamiliar with the law and may be in a particularly vulnerable situation due to whatever misfortune it was that led the attorney to seek him out. For these reasons, a prophylactic rule prohibiting solicitation serves sufficient state interests so as to pass First Amendment scrutiny. Affirmed.

ANALYSIS

At one time, states imposed a near categorical ban on much of the businesslike aspects of law, such as advertising and solicitation. Many of these prohibitions have been lifted after the United States Supreme Court began applying the First Amendment to attorney advertising. Solicitation is the one area that has not changed in this regard.

Quicknotes

COMMERCIAL SPEECH Any speech that proposes a commercial transaction, or promotes products or services.

PROHIBITION AGAINST IN-PERSON SOLICITATION Ethical limits placed on attorneys when seeking to enter into a client relationship, preventing attorney from engaging in coercive or improper behavior when contacting potential clients directly.

Zauderer v. Office of Disciplinary Counsel

Attorney (D) v. Ohio state bar (P)

471 U.S. 626 (1985)

NATURE OF CASE: Appeal from state's highest court decision ordering public reprimand of an attorney based on the attorney's advertisements.

FACT SUMMARY: Attorney Zauderer (D) placed in numerous newspapers an advertisement targeting as potential clients women who had used the Dalkon Shield Intrauterine Device, which was known to cause numerous health problems. The state's Office of Disciplinary Counsel (Office) (P) disciplined him on several grounds for doing so. Zauderer (D) contended that the state could not constitutionally restrict his truthful commercial speech or require that he disclose that clients could be liable for litigation costs.

RULE OF LAW

(1) A state may not prohibit a truthful, nonfraudulent legal service advertisement that does not concern unlawful activities merely because the advertisement contains information or advice regarding a specific legal problem.

(2) Illustrations in legal service advertisements are protected by the First Amendment from regulation where the illustrations are accurate and non-deceptive.

(3) States may constitutionally require that legal service advertisements fully disclose the terms of the type of engagement advertised.

FACTS: Attorney Zauderer (D) placed in 36 newspapers an advertisement identifying the "Dalkon Shield," an IUD, and inviting women who had used the device to contact his office about their legal rights. The ad informed the reader that the device had been found to cause various physical problems and that Zauderer's (D) office was handling a number of cases involving the Shield. The ad also informed the reader that cases were handled on a contingency fee basis, but failed to notify the reader that clients could be liable for legal costs (as opposed to fees) regardless of the success of their claim. The state Office of Disciplinary Counsel (Office) (P) filed a disciplinary action against Zauderer (D), contending that he had violated several state rules against solicitation. These regulations prohibited soliciting legal business through advertisements containing advice and information regarding specific legal problems; placed restrictions on the use of illustrations in advertising by lawyers; and required certain disclosures relating to the terms of contingent fees and litigation costs. The state's highest court upheld the Office's (P) imposition of discipline, ordering that Zauderer (D) be publicly reprimanded, and the United States Supreme Court granted certiorari.

ISSUE:

(1) May a state prohibit a truthful, nonfraudulent legal service advertisement that does not concern unlawful activities merely because the advertisement contains information or advice regarding a specific legal problem?
(2) Are illustrations in legal service advertisements protected by the First Amendment from regulation where the illustrations are accurate and non-deceptive?
(3) May states constitutionally require that legal service advertisements fully disclose the terms of the type of engagement advertised?

HOLDING AND DECISION: (White, J.)

(1) No. A state may not prohibit a truthful, nonfraudulent legal service advertisement that does not concern unlawful activities merely because the advertisement contains information or advice regarding a specific legal problem. This Court has held that government has an interest in prohibiting advertisement that is false, deceptive or misleading, or that concerns unlawful activities. However, when these interests are not implicated, the First Amendment protects commercial speech. Here, the Office (P) contended that Zauderer's (D) advertisement ran afoul of anti-solicitation rules. However, it is not clear how the advertisement in question violated these rules. There is no allegation that the ad is false or misleading; in fact, it is not disputed that it is quite accurate. An advertisement such as that at issue here carries none of the potentialities for coercion, overreaching, or intimidation that led this Court to approve of categorical bans on in-person solicitation. Also, there is no evidence that it will "stir up litigation." It is not stirring up litigation to notify people that they may have rights, and litigation undertaken to vindicate rights or redress injuries in good faith is not an evil. Finally, the Office's (P) premise, that it is intrinsically difficult to distinguish advertisements containing legal advice that is false or deceptive from those that are truthful and helpful, is unfounded. In essence, there is no substantial governmental interest that is advanced by a blanket ban on advertisements of this

Continued on next page.

type, so such a ban is unconstitutional. Reversed as to this issue.

(2) Yes. Illustrations in legal service advertisements are protected by the First Amendment from regulation where the illustrations are accurate and non-deceptive. The analysis regarding the illustration of the Dalkon Shield in Zauderer's (D) advertisement is similar to the analysis used to determine whether the government had a substantial interest in regulating the text of the ad. Provided the illustration is non-deceptive, accurate, and unlikely to confuse the reader, it is protected by the First Amendment notwithstanding that some readers might find it offensive or embarrassing. Also rejected is the Office's (P) argument that the use of illustrations in advertising by attorneys creates unacceptable risks that the public will be misled, manipulated, or confused; the Office (P) has failed to present convincing evidence that identifying deceptive or manipulative uses of visual media in advertising is so intrinsically burdensome that the state is entitled to forgo that task in favor of the more convenient but far more restrictive alternative of a blanket ban on the use of illustrations. Reversed as to this issue.

(3) Yes. States may constitutionally require that legal service advertisements fully disclose the terms of the type of engagement advertised. The analysis applied to the text and illustration in Zauderer's (D) ad is inapplicable to the requirement that he disclose the terms of his engagement. That is because, constitutionally speaking, there is a significant difference between outright bans on speech and requiring truthful disclosures. Because the extension of First Amendment protection to commercial speech is justified principally by the value to consumers of the information such speech provides, Zauderer's (D) constitutionally protected interest in not providing any particular factual information in his advertising is minimal. An advertiser's rights are adequately protected as long as disclosure requirements are reasonably related to the state's interest in preventing deception of consumers. The Office's (P) position that it is deceptive to employ advertising that refers to contingent-fee arrangements without mentioning the client's liability for costs is reasonable enough to support the disclosure requirement. Affirmed as to this issue.

DISSENT: (O'Connor, J.) [Justice O'Connor's dissent addressed that portion of the majority's opinion that dealt with the issue of whether a state may prohibit a truthful, nonfraudulent legal service advertisement that does not concern unlawful activities merely because the advertisement contains information or advice regarding a specific legal problem.] The use of unsolicited legal advice to entice clients poses enough of a risk of overreaching and undue influence to warrant the state's rule. First, because professional services are complex, there is a greater possibility of creating confusion and deception. Second, the attorney's self-interest in obtaining business may color the advice given, so that the public will potentially receive advice that is incomplete and/or self-serving. Accordingly, the state has a substantial interest in regulating such speech, and doing so will not reduce the avenues attorneys have for informing the public of their legal rights.

ANALYSIS

Legal advertising is commercial speech. Commercial speech enjoys a more limited protection under the First Amendment than most other types of speech. In most situations, the government must show a "compelling" interest to restrict speech. In commercial speech, the government must show a less burdensome "substantial" interest. Even under this standard, most cases involving attorney advertising in the last two decades have gone against the government.

Quicknotes

COMMERCIAL SPEECH Any speech that proposes a commercial transaction, or promotes products or services.

Glossary

Common Latin Words and Phrases Encountered in the Law

A FORTIORI: Because one fact exists or has been proven, therefore a second fact that is related to the first fact must also exist.

A PRIORI: From the cause to the effect. A term of logic used to denote that when one generally accepted truth is shown to be a cause, another particular effect must necessarily follow.

AB INITIO: From the beginning; a condition that has existed throughout, as in a marriage that was void ab initio.

ACTUS REUS: The wrongful act; in criminal law, such action as is sufficient to trigger criminal liability.

AD VALOREM: According to value; an ad valorem tax is imposed upon an item located within the taxing jurisdiction calculated by the value of such item.

AMICUS CURIAE: Friend of the court. Its most common usage takes the form of an amicus curiae brief, filed by a person who is not a party to an action but is nonetheless allowed to offer an argument supporting his or her legal interests.

ARGUENDO: In arguing. A statement, possibly hypothetical, made for the purpose of argument.

BILL QUIA TIMET: A bill to quiet title (establish ownership) to real property.

BONA FIDE: True, honest, or genuine. May refer to a person's legal position based on good faith or lacking notice of fraud (such as a bona fide purchaser for value) or to the authenticity of a particular document (such as a bona fide last will and testament).

CAUSA MORTIS: With approaching death in mind. A gift causa mortis is a gift given by a party who feels certain that death is imminent.

CAVEAT EMPTOR: Let the buyer beware. This maxim is reflected in the rule of law that a buyer purchases at his or her own risk because it is the buyer's responsibility to examine, judge, test, and otherwise inspect what he or she is buying.

CERTIORARI: A writ of review. Petitions for review of a case by the United States Supreme Court are most often done by means of a writ of certiorari.

CONTRA: On the other hand. Opposite. Contrary to.

CORAM NOBIS: Before us; a writ of error directed to the court that originally rendered the judgment.

CORAM VOBIS: Before you; a writ of error directed by an appellate court to a lower court to correct a factual error.

CORPUS DELICTI: The body of the crime; the requisite elements of a crime amounting to objective proof that a crime has been committed.

CUM TESTAMENTO ANNEXO, ADMINISTRATOR (ADMINISTRATOR C.T.A.): With will annexed; an administrator c.t.a. settles an estate pursuant to a will in which he or she is not appointed.

DE BONIS NON, ADMINISTRATOR (ADMINISTRATOR D.B.N.): Of goods not administered; an administrator d.b.n. settles a partially settled estate.

DE FACTO: In fact; in reality; actually. Existing in fact but not officially approved or engendered.

DE JURE: By right; lawful. Describes a condition that is legitimate "as a matter of law," in contrast to the term "de facto," which connotes something existing in fact but not legally sanctioned or authorized. For example, de facto segregation refers to segregation brought about by housing patterns, etc., whereas de jure segregation refers to segregation created by law.

DE MINIMUS: Of minimal importance; insignificant; a trifle; not worth bothering about.

DE NOVO: Anew; a second time; afresh. A trial de novo is a new trial held at the appellate level as if the case originated there and the trial at a lower level had not taken place.

DICTA: Generally used as an abbreviated form of obiter dicta, a term describing those portions of a judicial opinion incidental or not necessary to resolution of the specific question before the court. Such nonessential statements and remarks are not considered to be binding precedent.

DUCES TECUM: Refers to a particular type of writ or subpoena requesting a party or organization to produce certain documents in its possession.

EN BANC: Full bench. Where a court sits with all justices present rather than the usual quorum.

EX PARTE: For one side or one party only. An ex parte proceeding is one undertaken for the benefit of only one party, without notice to, or an appearance by, an adverse party.

EX POST FACTO: After the fact. An ex post facto law is a law that retroactively changes the consequences of a prior act.

EX REL.: Abbreviated form of the term "ex relatione," meaning upon relation or information. When the state brings an action in which it has no interest against an individual at the instigation of one who has a private interest in the matter.

FORUM NON CONVENIENS: Inconvenient forum. Although a court may have jurisdiction over the case, the action should be tried in a more conveniently located court, one to which parties and witnesses may more easily travel, for example.

GUARDIAN AD LITEM: A guardian appointed by the court to represent a minor or incompetent person in a legal action.

HABEAS CORPUS: You have the body. The modern writ of habeas corpus is a writ directing that a person (body) being detained (such as a prisoner) be brought before the court so that the legality of his or her detention can be judicially ascertained.

IN CAMERA: In private, in chambers. When a hearing is held before a judge in his or her chambers or when all spectators are excluded from the courtroom.

IN FORMA PAUPERIS: In the manner of a pauper. A party who proceeds in forma pauperis because of his or her poverty is one who is allowed to bring suit without liability for costs.

INFRA: Below, under. A word referring the reader to a later part of a book. (The opposite of supra.)

IN LOCO PARENTIS: In the place of a parent.

IN PARI DELICTO: Equally wrong; a court of equity will not grant requested relief to an applicant who is in pari delicto, or as much at fault in the transactions giving rise to the controversy as is the opponent of the applicant.

IN PARI MATERIA: On like subject matter or upon the same matter. Statutes relating to the same person or things are said to be in pari materia. It is a general rule of statutory construction that such statutes should be construed together, i.e., looked at as if they together constituted one law.

IN PERSONAM: Against the person. Jurisdiction over the person of an individual.

IN RE: In the matter of. Used to designate a proceeding involving an estate or other property.

IN REM: Signifies an action against the res, or thing. An action in rem is basically one that is taken directly against property, as distinguished from an action in personam, i.e., against the person.

INTER ALIA: Among other things. Used to show that the whole of a statement, pleading, list, statute, etc., has not been set forth in its entirety.

INTER PARTES: Between the parties. May refer to contracts, conveyances, or other transactions having legal significance.

INTER VIVOS: Between the living. An inter vivos gift is a gift made by a living grantor, as distinguished from bequests contained in a will, which pass upon the death of the testator.

IPSO FACTO: By the mere fact itself.

JUS: Law or the entire body of law.

LEX LOCI: The law of the place; the notion that the rights of parties to a legal proceeding are governed by the law of the place where those rights arose.

MALUM IN SE: Evil or wrong in and of itself; inherently wrong. Describes an act that is wrong by its very nature, as opposed to one which would not be wrong but for the fact that there is a specific legal prohibition against it (malum prohibitum).

MALUM PROHIBITUM: Wrong because prohibited, but not inherently evil. Describes something that is wrong because it is expressly forbidden by law but that is not in and of itself evil, e.g., speeding.

MANDAMUS: We command. A writ directing an official to take a certain action.

MENS REA: A guilty mind; a criminal intent. A term used to signify the mental state that accompanies a crime or other prohibited act. Some crimes require only a general mens rea (general intent to do the prohibited act), but others, like assault with intent to murder, require the existence of a specific mens rea.

MODUS OPERANDI: Method of operating; generally refers to the manner or style of a criminal in committing crimes, admissible in appropriate cases as evidence of the identity of a defendant.

NEXUS: A connection to.

NISI PRIUS: A court of first impression. A nisi prius court is one where issues of fact are tried before a judge or jury.

N.O.V. (NON OBSTANTE VEREDICTO): Notwithstanding the verdict. A judgment n.o.v. is a judgment given in favor of one party despite the fact that a verdict was returned in favor of the other party, the justification being that the verdict either had no reasonable support in fact or was contrary to law.

NUNC PRO TUNC: Now for then. This phrase refers to actions that may be taken and will then have full retroactive effect.

PENDENTE LITE: Pending the suit; pending litigation underway.

PER CAPITA: By head; beneficiaries of an estate, if they take in equal shares, take per capita.

PER CURIAM: By the court; signifies an opinion ostensibly written "by the whole court" and with no identified author.

PER SE: By itself, in itself; inherently.

PER STIRPES: By representation. Used primarily in the law of wills to describe the method of distribution where a person, generally because of death, is unable to take that which is left to him or her by the will of another, and therefore his or her heirs divide such property between them rather than take under the will individually.

PRIMA FACIE: On its face, at first sight. A prima facie case is one that is sufficient on its face, meaning that the evidence supporting it is adequate to establish the case until contradicted or overcome by other evidence.

PRO TANTO: For so much; as far as it goes. Often used in eminent domain cases when a property owner receives partial payment for his or her land without prejudice to his or her right to bring suit for the full amount he or she claims the land to be worth.

QUANTUM MERUIT: As much as the party deserves. Refers to recovery based on the doctrine of unjust enrichment in those cases in which a party has rendered valuable services or furnished materials that were accepted and enjoyed by another under circumstances that would reasonably notify the recipient that the rendering party expected to be paid. In essence, the law implies a contract to pay the reasonable value of the services or materials furnished.

QUASI: Almost like; as if; nearly. Essentially used to signify that one subject or thing is almost analogous to another but that material differences between them do exist. For example, a quasi-criminal proceeding is one that is not strictly criminal but shares enough of the same characteristics to require some of the same safeguards (e.g., procedural due process must be followed in a parole hearing).

QUID PRO QUO: Something for something. In contract law, the consideration, something of value, passed between the parties to render the contract binding.

RES GESTAE: Things done. In evidence law, this principle justifies the admission of a statement that would otherwise be hearsay when it is made so closely to the event in question as to be said to be a part of it, or with such spontaneity as not to have the possibility of falsehood.

RES IPSA LOQUITUR: The thing speaks for itself. This doctrine gives rise to a rebuttable presumption of negligence when the instrumentality causing the injury was within the exclusive control of the defendant, and the injury was one that does not normally occur unless a person has been negligent.

RES JUDICATA: A matter adjudged. Doctrine that provides that once a court of competent jurisdiction has rendered a final judgment or decree on the merits, that judgment or decree is conclusive upon the parties to the case and prevents them from engaging in any other litigation on the points and issues determined therein.

RESPONDEAT SUPERIOR: Let the master reply. This doctrine holds the master liable for the wrongful acts of his or her servant (or the principal for his or her agent) in those cases in which the servant (or agent) was acting within the scope of his or her authority at the time of the injury.

STARE DECISIS: To stand by or adhere to that which has been decided. The common-law doctrine of stare decisis attempts to give security and certainty to the law by following the policy that once a principle of law as applicable to a certain set of facts has been set forth in a decision, it forms a precedent that will subsequently be followed, even though a different decision might be made were it the first time the question had arisen. Of course, stare decisis is not an inviolable principle and is departed from in instances where there is good cause (e.g., considerations of public policy led the Supreme Court to disregard prior decisions sanctioning segregation).

SUPRA: Above. A word referring a reader to an earlier part of a book. (The opposite of infra.)

ULTRA VIRES: Beyond the power. This phrase is most commonly used to refer to actions taken by a corporation that are beyond the power or legal authority of the corporation.

Addendum of French Derivatives

CHATTEL: Tangible personal property.

CY PRES: Doctrine permitting courts to apply trust funds to purposes not expressed in the trust but necessary to carry out the settlor's intent.

IN PAIS: Not pursuant to legal proceedings.

PER AUTRE VIE: For another's life; during another's life. In property law, an estate may be granted that will terminate upon the death of someone other than the grantee.

PROFIT A PRENDRE: A license to remove minerals or other produce from land.

VOIR DIRE: Process of questioning jurors as to their predispositions about the case or parties to a proceeding in order to identify those jurors displaying bias or prejudice.

www.ingramcontent.com/pod-product-compliance
Lightning Source LLC
LaVergne TN
LVHW082354200926
848481LV00012B/3561
9798889069645